JAMES J. CONKLIN, M.D.
Chairman & CEO

Quick Reference to Computer Graphics Terms

Quick Reference to Computer Graphics Terms

ROGER T. STEVENS

ACADEMIC PRESS PROFESSIONAL

A Division of Harcourt Brace & Company

Boston   San Diego   New York
London   Sydney   Tokyo   Toronto

ACADEMIC PRESS PROFESSIONAL
955 Massachusetts Avenue, Cambridge, MA 02139

An Imprint of ACADEMIC PRESS, INC.
A Division of HARCOURT BRACE & COMPANY

United Kingdom Edition published by
ACADEMIC PRESS LIMITED
24–28 Oval Road, London NW1 7DX

ISBN: 0-12-668310-7
LCCCN: 93-72453

Printed in the United States of America
93 94 95 96 EB 9 8 7 6 5 4 3 2 1

Preface

Every time I get a new issue of a computer magazine, I read about another great step forward in computer graphics, particularly in the capabilities available for creating lifelike pictures on the successors to the simple and affordable IBM personal computer. Along with these descriptions of wonderful capabilities, each time I am introduced to a number of new acronyms and phrases that have specialized graphics meanings. The number of unique graphics terms is now so great that even those who are most expert in graphics are constantly running across terms that are out of their particular field of expertise and therefore unfamiliar. Certainly the computer graphics field is in dire need of a quick reference guide that collects the meanings of graphics terms in a convenient reference volume.

Any reader that uses such a quick reference will sooner or later come up with one or both of two questions. First, why isn't this term that I am looking for in the volume? Second, why is this term that I came across in the volume at all? It doesn't look like a graphics term to me. These questions precisely identify the problem of the author, which is what should and should not appear in the volume. Rather than attempt to make any defense of what is and what is not in this book, I am simply going to describe how it was put together.

I currently have in my library 42 books on computer graphics. I began by listing every word and phrase that appeared in the indexes and glossaries of these books. I then went over this list, searching for definitions of these terms and also attempting to make some judgment as to which of them were directly enough related to graphics so that they should be part of the book and which should not be included. For definitions, I most often went back to the book that described the term. Usually I had to come up with a definition in my own words, since many highly technical authors leave something to be desired in explaining terms simply. Sometimes I went back to *Webster's Dictionary* to find what they thought a word meant, although usually the *Webster's* definition is quite different from the generally accepted technical meaning. A few terms appeared in some other graphics dictionary, which made it easier to come up with an acceptable definition, although I didn't always agree with the other authors. I also have a good collection of math books for attempting to decipher math terminology and a communications dictionary and some books on radio and radar that were occasionally useful. Finally, my publishers had at least two editors go over the manuscript and make comments, which I incorporated into the final version.

So what if you are looking for a term and it isn't in this volume? First, it may be a term that I never heard of and that wasn't used by any of my 42 reference authors. If so, I'd like to hear about it and get it into the next edition. Second, it may be a term so new that I haven't heard it yet. If it becomes current, you'll see it in the next edition, but just in case I miss it, I'd still like to hear from you. The third possibility is that even though you think that the missing term is the most important one in computer graphics, I have already considered it and decided that it didn't have a place in this volume. In that case, one protest isn't likely to change my mind (unless accompanied by a very strong argument), but several protests might induce me to include it in the next edition.

What about that term that you think is just out of place and shouldn't be in the book at all? It must have occurred in at least one of my references, and if the connection to graphics isn't clear to you, it was to me and to the original author of the reference book. I'm not likely to remove it, but I could be induced to clarify the connection.

Finally, a word about definitions. I take full responsibility for all the definitions in the book. If they are incorrect, or unclear, or too short, or too long, it's my fault. Please bear in mind, however, that this is not a textbook nor an encyclopedia. You are not expected to have a complete understanding of the intricacies of a term after reading its definition in this book. You are expected to know what is meant by the term and to have achieved enough understanding to decide whether you need to get more detailed knowledge from a comprehensive reference text. Dictionary definitions are supposed to be simple and understandable. At least, I've tried. If you have a major gripe about any definition, I would appreciate hearing from you. Sarcastic comments don't help much, however. Tell me what you think I should have said.

This book is about three times as big as any list of graphics terms that I have seen elsewhere, so hopefully you'll have a better chance of finding the term that you are looking for. At the rate at which the field is changing, it will have to be updated fairly often. Maybe each new edition will be better than the last.

A

abend. **Ab**normal **end**. End of a program in other than the desired manner. Some types of programming or hardware errors permit the program to stop and report an error message that may give clues as to what went wrong. Other types of error cause a *system crash*, where the system locks up and must be manually reset, often causing loss of data.

ABI. Applications binary interface. Low-level interface specifications for a graphics or software system.

ablate. To remove. Optical disks are written by ablating material from the disk surface with a laser beam, forming pits which can be read.

abscissa. The horizontal or x component of a two-dimensional coordinate system. The vertical or y component is the *ordinate*.

absolute. 1. In geometry, specified with respect to a fixed origin. For example, when a set of coordinates is given with respect to the origin of the coordinate system rather than with respect to the previous point specified. 2. In algebra, the numerical part of a number, irrespective of sign. For example *-3* and *+3* both have an absolute value of *3*.

absolute address. In computing, the address of the memory location where a datum is stored, referenced to the beginning of memory (address 0). Compare with *relative address*.

absolute coordinates. A coordinate system for defining the positions of objects in a scene to be rendered that is independent of the display screen or the objects within the scene. In contrast, the position of an object may be defined relative to the observer, the display screen, or some other object for convenience during the rendering process.

absolute pseudoprime. A number defined by $N | (b^{N-1} - 1)$ for all $(\mathbf{b},\mathbf{N})$ = **1**. The smallest absolute pseudoprime is $561 = 3 \times 11 \times 17$. Also known as a *Carmichael number*.

absolute temperature. The temperature at which all molecular activity ceases. This is -273° centigrade. The kelvin temperature scale is defined with 0°K as the absolute temperature and each degree having the same magnitude as a centigrade degree, so that a kelvin temperature is the same as a centigrade temperature with 273 added to it.

absolute value. In algebra, the numerical part of a number, irrespective of sign. For example *-3* and *+3* both have an absolute value of *3*.

absorption. Act or process of being taken in. Particularly of concern in graphic renditions because certain light frequencies can be absorbed by certain otherwise transparent materials, thereby causing the light color to change.

absorption coefficient. The fraction of incident intensity of light absorbed by a material per unit of thickness for small thicknesses.

abstract concrete. Proposed fractal structure of concrete suggested by David Jones, in which proper arrangement of particles sized from coarse gravel to the finest dust can be used to reduce the needed binder to an arbitrarily small amount, thereby reducing cost.

a-buffering. A variation of the *z-buffering* technique which facilitates *antialiasing*. The z-buffer is a two-dimensional array of height values. Each *z-buffer* value, together with its array dimensions, defines a point on a three-dimensional surface. The *a-buffer* uses the same type of array, but instead of each element containing a height, it contains a pointer to a stack of data that not only defines the current point but also surrounding ones, so that the proper color value for antialiasing may be computed.

acceleration. The rate of change of velocity of a body that is changing speed, direction, or both. In graphics, often used to refer to hardware or software techniques used to speed up graphics operations.

accelerator board. 1. Plug-in board for a computer that speeds up operations by using a more powerful microprocessor or some similar means. 2. A plug-in board specifically designed to speed up video operations, either by improving the speed of memory access or by providing a special processor that performs primitive operations such as line or shape drawing faster than could be done by the computer microprocessor.

accelerator port. In a graphics accelerator card, the I/O port that receives data for processing by the card, as opposed to the *direct frame buffer port*, which permits bypassing the accelerator card and passing video data directly to the display memory.

acceptance test procedure. A formal document describing a series of tests which a system or software package must pass in order to be accepted (and paid for) by the customer.

access method. The manner in which data are stored and retrieved. This is highly dependent upon the media used. Tape units usually store all data in a sequential stream. Disk drives are divided into sectors (often of 512 bytes), any one of which may be accessed by the computer. This gives a lot of flexibility but has the drawback that after awhile a file may be broken up into a lot of individual sectors spread across the disk, resulting in what is known as *fragmenting*, which slows disk access considerably. Any byte of a RAM can be accessed directly. The speed with which a particular datum can be accessed may be critical in such applications as transferring data to the display screen fast enough to produce satisfactory moving pictures.

accessible boundary point. A point p on the boundary of an open set W for which there is a path beginning in W such that p is the first point not in W which the path hits.

accommodation. 1. The automatic adjustment of the eye to permit focusing at different distances. 2. The range of distances over which the eye can focus.

accumulation. Process in plants where the increase or decrease in certain cell components is measured to determine when flowering will begin. This is one method of modeling plant growth so as to know when to begin constructing blossoms.

accumulation point. A starting point in the complex plane for an iterated equation to which the solution of the equation returns periodically during the iteration process.

acetate-base film. Photographic film in which the emulsion is laid down on an acetate substrate. Acetate is one of the substrate materials which meets ANSI safety standards (particularly in that it does not burn rapidly).

achromatic. 1. Colorless, thus comprised only of black, white, and shades of gray. Also referred to as monochrome. 2. The ability of a lens to focus two or more different colors at the same point.

acknowledgment. A computer output indicating that a particular piece of information has been successfully received.

ACM. Association for Computing Machinery. Society for those involved professionally with computer hardware or software. Located at 1515 Broadway, New York, NY 10036.

acoustic tablet. A device for detecting the position of a stylus on a tablet and converting it to a pair of *(x,y)* coordinate electrical signals. Strip microphones are used on the horizontal and vertical edges of the tablet to detect sound emitted by the stylus. The time of travel of the sound to each microphone is measured to determine the stylus position. This technique is particularly adaptable to three-dimensional space measurements. By adding a third strip microphone at right angles to the other two, the position of the stylus in a cube of space can be determined.

actinic. A chemical change (particularly in a light-sensitive photographic emulsion) produced by the shorter wavelengths (such as violet or ultraviolet rays).

active array. A group of loudspeakers, radio antennas, radar antennas, or television antennas whose characteristics of beam width and direction can be controlled by proper phasing of the drive to the individual units.

active bank. In PCs, normally 64K (65536) of computer memory addresses are allowed for display memory. Super VGA cards often have more memory than will fit in this addressing space (even using the 4 bank EGA/VGA memory configuration). Consequently the super VGA display memory is divided into 64K banks, only one of which is mapped to the computer addressing space at any given time. This bank is known as the *active bank*. Reading and writing can only be done to the active bank.

active character sets. The IBM PC may have a number of character sets resident in its Basic Input/Output System (BIOS). These are stored in read-only memory (ROM) in the computer. At any one time, two of these character sets may be selected for display. The selected character sets are known as the *active character sets*.

active data base. In flight simulators, the portion of the graphics data base which is kept in random access memory (RAM) so as to be quickly accessible to the graphics display.

active display area. That portion of the display screen upon which pixels can be changed in color and intensity to produce a desired display. Most computer monitors have areas around the edges of the screen which cannot be accessed and therefore are not part of the active display. In addition, a border around the active display area is colored with a selected background color and cannot otherwise be modified.

active edge list. A list used in scan conversion techniques. As the scan line scrolls in the y direction, the *active edge list* contains x values for each line that straddles the active scan line.

active matrix LCD. An LCD display in which each monochrome pixel or each red, green, and blue dot making up a color pixel is controlled by a discrete transistor. (These transistors are all incorporated in an integrated circuit.) This technique, while using more transistors than a standard LCD display, permits sharper contrast, increased writing and screen access speeds, and eliminates loss of cursor (submarining).

active page. The display memory for the IBM PC EGA or VGA card may be configured to have from 1 to 8 pages of full screen graphics, depending upon the display mode and the amount of memory on the card. Only one page at a time may be selected for display. The selected page is called the *active page*.

active subtree. In ray-tracing constructive solid geometry (CSG) images, the part of the CSG tree which contributes to the image for each scan line.

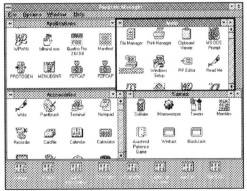

active window. The window that is at the front of the screen when several programs are being run simultaneously in the Windows environment. All input from the keyboard will be directed to this window. A window is made *active* by placing the mouse cursor on any part of it and clicking.

Active Window (at upper right)

activity network. A chart used in project planning which utilizes boxes containing summaries of tasks and lines connecting the boxes to show the order in which the tasks must be performed.

actuator. Mechanical device that moves an object, such as the voice coil or stepping switch that positions the read/write head of a disk drive.

Adams-Bashforth method.   A technique for solving differential equations, used to graph the Verhulst attractor fractal.

adaptation. The ability of the brain to vary the size of the pupil of the eye and to chemically vary the sensitivity of the retina so as to adjust the eye's sensitivity to light over a wide range of light intensities.

adapter, video. A printed circuit card that plugs into an IBM PC or clone to provide the interface to a video monitor. Four commonly used video adapters are the Monochrome Display Adapter (MDA), which displays monochrome text only with no graphics at a resolution of 720×350 pixels; the Color Graphics Array (CGA), which displays 4-color graphics at 320×200 pixels and higher resolution text; the Enhanced Graphics Array (EGA), which displays 16-color graphics at a resolution of 640×350 pixels and also lower resolution and text modes, and the Video Graphics Adapter (VGA), which displays 16 colors at 640×480 pixels, 256 colors at 320×200 pixels, as well as all the EGA modes.

adaptive compression. A data compression technique that continually analyzes the data content and modifies the compression algorithm to achieve near-optimum compression ratios. The Lempel Ziv Welch technique used in creating GIF graphics files is a good example of this.

adaptive division graph. A technique used in ray tracing in which the space to be ray traced is subdivided using an octree containing voxels (elements of volume) of varying size based on distribution of objects in the space and then each voxel has attached to it a quadtree for the neighbor of each face.

adaptive forward differencing. A technique for rendering images on curved surfaces that uses the surface, viewpoint, and display resolution information to determine the amount of detail needed for the image and adjusts the number of points computed accordingly.

adaptive meshing. Technique for breaking a picture up into patches whose size is inversely proportional to intensity variations when generating a picture using the radiosity method.

adaptive sampling. Method of sampling in which the sampling density of a parameter is controlled by use of a quality estimate.

adaptive subdivision. A technique for adjusting the sizes of polygons that make up a mesh representing a curved surface, the size of each polygon being determined by its projected size or by the local curvature of the curved surface or both.

adaptive supersampling. A technique used in ray tracing, which begins by tracing five rays through the center and four corners of a pixel. If they are found to be of about the same color, the pixel is colored that color; if they differ significantly in color, the pixel is subdivided into smaller regions and the process repeated.

adaptive tree-depth control. A technique which causes a ray-tracing system to stop tracing a ray when its contributions to the color of the ultimate eye ray fall below some selected threshold.

ADB. Apple Desktop Bus. Plug-in port on the Apple Macintosh computer for connection of the keyboard, mouse, trackball, etc.

A/D converter. Analog-to-digital converter. A device for converting a voltage level into a digital number consisting of a series of bits that represents the level. A digital voltmeter, for example, accepts a voltage level input, passes it through an analog-to-digital converter, and displays a number representing the voltage. A voltage having a level of 412 volts would be converted to the binary number 11001110, which is equivalent to the decimal number 412.

additive color synthesis. Combining light of the primary colors red, green, and blue to produce light of a desired color, as opposed to subtractive color synthesis in which white light is absorbed by pigments of crimson, yellow, and light blue, leaving the unabsorbed component as the apparent color of the object.

address. 1. A number that identifies a particular location of a memory storage device, such as random access memory (RAM) or disk. 2. As a verb, to select a specified memory location.

addressability. The ability to place information at a certain location in memory. Particularly important in PC graphics, where the addressing space available is much smaller than the amount of memory needed for displaying in many graphics modes. Sixteen color modes assign each pixel to a bit of memory at a particular address, but the color of the pixel actually contains four bits of data, so the graphics adapter card contains four memory planes. Each of the four bits must be written to its proper plane using the same memory address, but sending the proper commands to internal registers so that the bit goes to the correct plane. For 256 and higher color modes, the required number of bits to define the color of each pixel is addressed adjacent in memory to the next pixel, but when the end of the assigned video memory space (usually 64K) is reached, a page register must be accessed to switch the page of memory that is currently addressed by the computer.

addressable capacity. The total number of memory locations that a computer can access. For personal computers, each location usually contains one byte (eight bits) of information. When addressing display memory, 16-color EGA/VGA display modes contain information for the color of eight pixels at one memory address. The four bits that represent one of sixteen colors are one bit in each of four display memory planes which are at the same computer address, the four planes being accessed internally by the display card. For 256-color VGA modes, a memory address contains the data for the color of one pixel.

addressing modes. Ways of addressing computer memory. When using assembly language, the three basic addressing modes are *immediate addressing*, which refers to the exact memory location; *indirect addressing*, which refers to a register that contains a pointer to a memory location; and *indexed addressing*, which allows the programmer to add an offset to the indirect address.

adjacent facets. Two facets of a polygonal solid which have a common edge.

adjoint matrices. If A_{ij} is the cofactor of the determinant $|a|$ of a square matrix $[a_{ij}]$, the matrix $[A_{ji}]$ is the adjoint of $[a_{ij}]$. The *adjoint matrix* has some special properties; for example , multiplication of it by the original matrix is commutative, which is not generally true of matrix multiplication. As an example, the adjoint of the matrix

$$[a_{ij}] = \begin{bmatrix} 2 & 0 & 7 \\ -1 & 4 & 5 \\ 3 & 1 & 2 \end{bmatrix}$$

is the matrix

$$[A_{ji}] = \begin{bmatrix} 3 & 7 & -28 \\ 17 & -17 & -17 \\ -13 & -2 & 8 \end{bmatrix}$$

To see how the elements of this second matrix are obtained, we note, for example, that the cofactor of a_{11} (2) is

$$\begin{bmatrix} 4 & 5 \\ 1 & 2 \end{bmatrix}$$

which evaluates to (4×2) - (1×5) = 3, which is thus the value for A_{ji}.

Adobe Illustrator. Software from Adobe Systems, Inc., Mountain View, CA, which is used to paint pictures on a computer screen.

Adobe Type Manager. Software from Adobe Systems, Inc., Mountain View, CA, which defines typefaces using Bezier curves plus various hints that enable a printer to produce PostScript type fonts of various sizes and rotations on the fly without jagged edges.

ADSTAR. Automatic Document Storage and Retrieval. A system that can select and display electronically stored images that meet some user criteria.

AFD. Adaptive forward differencing. A technique for rendering images of curved surfaces that varies the resolution in rendering so as to obtain the same amount of detail as the viewpoint and surface orientation change, thereby minimizing the necessary computer computations.

affine map. An array of information defining transformations that consist only of translations, rotations, scalings, and shears. Also known as an *affine matrix*.

affine transformation. A transformation that consists only of translations, rotations, scalings, and shears. The array of information that defines the *affine transformation* is usually stored in an *affine matrix*. This type of transformation is particularly important in creating fractal representations of pictures using iterated function systems.

AFP. AppleTalk Filing Protocol. A protocol used by non-Apple networks to access data from an AppleTalk server.

aggregate object. An object defined by a collection of primitives such as facets, parallelograms, circles, etc.

Aida. Gate-level simulation accelerator software used for the simulation of LSI logic gate-array designs. A product of Teredyne, Inc.

AIIM. Association for Information and Image Management. A professional society for those involved with micrographics, optical disks, and electronic image management. Located at 1100 Wayne Ave., Suite 1100, Silver Spring, MD 20910. Phone 301-587-8202.

aiming symbol. Symbol such as a circle that appears on a display to serve as a tracking point for a light pen.

air resistance. Opposition to a moving body imposed by the earth's atmosphere. An important factor in modeling of aircraft and missile trajectories.

AIX. A version of the UNIX operating system developed by IBM.

Albers' equal-area conic map projection. Method of projecting a portion of a sphere or ellipsoid onto a two-dimensional map in a way that minimizes distortion. The method intersects a cone with a hemisphere so that there are two circles of intersection, each at a constant latitude. The hemisphere is then projected onto the cone and the cone unrolled to produce a map.

Aldus Pagemaker. A program used for desktop publishing. Developed by Aldus Corp., 411 First Ave. South, Suite 200, Seattle, WA 98104.

algebraic behavior. Behavior of a function that can be characterized by two simple power laws with exponents 1 and -1 respectively.

algebraic irrational numbers. The set of algebraic numbers that cannot be expressed as the ratio of two integers.

algebraic numbers. The set of all positive and negative numbers.

algebraic surface. A surface which is the locus of points defined when a given algebraic function is set equal to a constant (frequently zero).

algorithm. A rule or procedure for solving a problem. It consists of a series of steps, usually in the form of a set of mathematical equations, for accomplishing a logical or mathematical process in an unambiguous manner. A particular instance may be implemented by software or specialized hardware.

algorithm, Cohen-Sutherland. Algorithm used for clipping lines that extend beyond the bounds of a specified window. The algorithm defines the world into nine regions, one being the specified window and the others above, below, to the right, and to the left of the window and combinations of these. Each region is assigned a unique four-bit number, which is used in processing the line endpoints.

alias. 1. A name that can be used to replace another name. In C programming, the #*define* statement can be used to create aliases. For example, #*define T TEST* would allow you to uses *T* instead of *TEST* anywhere in the program. 2. Electronic mail distribution list of addresses for a particular topic.

aliased line. A line consisting of stair steps as the result of attempting to draw a slanting line as an aggregate of points from a grid of limited resolution.

aliasing. The visual result of producing an image by sampling an image at a sample frequency lower than the highest spatial frequencies contained in the image. This occurs when a real scene is reduced to the number of samples dictated by the available pixels on a display screen. The effects include stairstepping of surface edges, breakup of thin lines into dots, and moire patterns in finely detailed areas.

alignment. 1. To arrange objects in a straight line. 2. To adjust a device or its parts so that the proper conditions exist for optimum operation. 3. For color cathode-ray tubes, the positioning of the electron beams from the red, blue, and green electron guns of the tube so that a group of red, green, and blue phosphor dots are activated to produce light at exactly the same place on the screen.

alignment error. Error in positioning of the electron beams of the red, green, and blue electron guns of a color cathode-ray tube. It is measured as the mean distance between centers of color spot pairs (R-G, R-B, and G-B) and is also known as *misconvergence.*

all points addressable. An array in which every cell can be individually addressed.

Allegro. Software for printed circuit board layout developed by Valid Logic, Inc.

allocate. To reserve amounts of a resource such as memory or disk that are required for a particular application.

allometry. The property of a tree that there is a relationship between the length of a point on a branch measured from the base of the tree and the diameter of the branch at that point. For many trees, when this length changes by r, the branch diameter changes by $r^{3/2}$.

all-1s problem. A classical problem that can be expressed in the language of cellular automata. Each square on an $n \times n$ chessboard is equipped with a light and a switch that reverses the state (on or off) of the neighboring (the square itself and its four edge-adjacent neighbors) lights. The problem is to start with a completely dark chessboard and find which switches must be activated to light up all bulbs.

alpha blending. Use of information in an alpha buffer to modify the color information of an image.

alpha buffer. A plane that contains image information, whether or not it is physically located in the same frame buffer that holds the color information for the image. Also known as a *depth buffer.*

alpha channel. The memory used to store the value or occlusion mask representing the fractional coverage of a pixel. Can be used along with color video information to ease the composing of video images.

alpha compositing operator. An operator used in an alpha buffer to modify image color information. Assuming two color vectors, A and B, that are modified by alpha compositing operators F_A and F_B, if both operators are 0, the result is completely transparent, if F_A is 1 and F_B is 0 the new color is A only, if F_A is 0 and F_B is 1 the new color is B only, and for other combinations of the operators various mixtures of the two colors occur.

alpha test. Test of a new product, particularly software, at a point when obvious problems have been fixed, but there hasn't been adequate debugging to make the product robust enough for public distribution. An *internal alpha test* is performed by users within the developing organization; an *external alpha test* allows selected users outside the organization to try the product. See also *beta test*.

alphageometric. Being drawn with graphics primitives rather than by using character symbols.

alphamosaic. Being formed with character symbols rather than drawn with graphics primitives.

alphanumeric. 1. A character that is either a letter of the alphabet or a number. 2. A character that is not a control character (such as form feed, carriage return, line feed, etc.) nor part of a control sequence. May be a letter, a number, or a punctuation mark.

alphanumeric COM. A computer output format which is limited to letters of the alphabet, numbers, and punctuation marks. Not capable of handling raster or vector graphics.

alphanumeric display. A computer display which can show only alphanumeric characters.

alternate color maps. Fractal pictures, such as Mandelbrot sets are usually created by assigning sequential colors (within the limits of color capability of the display system) to represent the number of times the base equation is iterated before it reaches some limit. However, other ways of assigning the colors give strikingly different pictures that give new insights into the fractal nature and structure. Each different way of assigning colors to create a fractal is known as an *alternate color map*.

alternate color option. A capability offered by the FRACTINT fractal generating program, which permits two variations of a fractal to be generated using shades of red for one and shades of blue for the other, so as to permit three-dimensional viewing using a special set of glasses.

ambient light. Nondirectional light that illuminates objects in a scene as result of scattered reflection. In an outdoor scene, this light comes from the hemisphere of blue sky and is approximately 20% of the intensity of direct sunlight. In modeling scenes with a computer, an ambient light term is usually applied to every object rendered.

ambiguity function. In radar, a function of range and range rate that vanishes everywhere except at one sharp function, thereby eliminating ambiguous radar signals that might be confused with the real target.

amicable number. One of a pair of numbers for which the sum of the divisors of one of a pair of amicable numbers equals the other amicable number and vice versa.

ammonia. A common chemical used in the processing of diazo film. It alkalizes the acidic elements of an exposed diazo coating, leaving the image on the paper. Xerography has largely replaced diazo processing except for very large drawings.

amorphous solid. A solid whose atoms are randomly distributed.

analglyph 3-D drawing. A drawing using red and blue pixels to produce a picture that appears three-dimensional when viewed through a pair of glasses in which one lens is red and the other blue.

analog. The representation of data or physical quantities by a continuous signal whose instantaneous amplitude is a function of the value of the data or physical quantity that the signal represents. For example, the instantaneous amplitude of the voltage produced by a sensor to represent the speed of rotation of a shaft would be considered an *analog* signal. Contrast to *digital*, which represents data or physical quantities by binary numbers. In the example given above, the *digital* representation would be in terms of a series of numbers representing the value at various sampling points.

analog computer. A computer in which variables used to represent data are continuous rather than discrete. An *analog computer* can, for example, use electric voltages and currents to represent quantities that vary continuously. Components of an analog computer consist of circuits that perform simple mathematical functions on the analog signals, such as summation, multiplication, division, differentiation, or integration. These components are connected in series as needed to apply a desired mathematical equation to the incoming data. *Analog computers* are limited in accuracy by the precision of the parts used in the circuits; by changes in part characteristics caused by temperature, humidity, pressure, or aging; and by variations in the supply voltages.

analog RGB monitor. A color computer monitor which accepts and displays red, green, and blue signals of any amplitude from zero to some maximum level. This permits creation of an unlimited number of different colors, whereas a digital monitor, which accepts just a few levels of each color, is severely limited in the number of colors it can produce. On the other hand, producing signals from a digital computer to drive an analog monitor is much more complicated than producing driving signals for a digital monitor. EGA monitors are digital monitors. VGA monitors (and television sets) are analog monitors.

analog-to-digital converter. A device for converting a voltage level into a digital number consisting of a series of bits that represents the level. A digital voltmeter, for example, accepts a voltage level input, passes it through an analog-to-digital converter, and displays a number representing the voltage. A voltage of 412 volts would be converted to the binary number 11001110, which is equivalent to the decimal number 412.

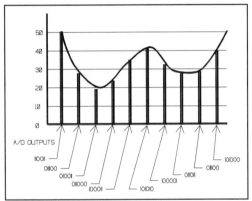

Analog-to-Digital Converter

anamorphic image.   1. An image that is unequally scaled in the horizontal and vertical dimensions. 2. A distorted image frequently used in movie formats (such as Panavision) where the width field of a wide angle picture is compressed into a 35-mm frame and the process is optically reversed on projection to give a wide-screen display.

anastomosis.   Branch reconnection that may take place between the veins of a leaf. Important in modeling plant structures.

AND.   Normally written in all caps, although not an acronym, to distinguish that it is a logic function. 1. A logic function whose output contains a one in every bit position where each of two inputs contained a one. 2. To perform the AND function.

Anderson localization. A lack of diffusion in certain disordered systems, which can be exactly solved through the use of the Bethe lattice.

Anderson Report, The. Monthly newsletter on computer graphics, specializing in graphics industry company business actions and new graphics products.

anechoic environment. A volume in which no reflections of waves exist.

angle increment. In turtle geometry, the angle through which the turtle is turned in response to a + or - command.

angle of incidence. The acute angle between a ray that is incident to the surface of an object and the surface normal at the point of intersection with the surface.

angle of reflection. The acute angle between a ray that is reflected from the surface of an object at the point where an incident ray intersects the surface and the surface normal at the point of intersection.

angle of refraction. The acute angle between a ray transmitted through an object from the surface and the surface normal at the point of origin of the ray.

angular deflection.   The displacement of points in rotational transformation in which each point at a specified distance from the origin is deflected by a specified angle.

angular distortion. The variation in appearance of an object as the viewing distance is changed, due to the characteristics of the human eye. Too large a viewing distance makes the object appear flat. Too small a viewing distance makes the object appear distorted and overly angular.

angular momentum. The momentum of a mass m moving with a speed v in a circle of radius r. The angular momentum is mvr. An important factor in creating animated displays of particle or planet orbits.

angular velocity. The speed at which a body is rotating, usually expressed in revolutions per some time unit, such as revolutions per second or revolutions per minute. An important factor in creating animated displays of particle or planet orbits.

animation. 1. A graphic method that creates the illusion of motion by rapid viewing of individual frames in a sequence. 2. The use of computer graphics to prepare sequences of frames for simulating motion. Because not all parts of a frame change from one frame in the sequence to the next, the amount of memory required can be much less than would be required for the same number of independent pictures.

animation, double-framed order. A technique for recording an animation by recording each even-numbered frame twice and dropping the odd-numbered frames. When displayed, the resulting animation makes animation errors more obvious.

anisotropic reflection. A variation in the index of refraction in birefringent crystals with direction of an impinging light beam, produced by the orderly arrangement of the atoms in the crystalline lattice.

anisotropic transformation. A mapping that doesn't preserve the original ratio of the x (horizontal) and y (vertical) components, thereby transforming squares to rectangles and circles to ovals. This often occurs unintentionally when computer graphics displays that don't use square pixels are used. It is then necessary to provide correction so that pictures will be accurate representations.

anisotropy. The exhibiting of properties with different values when measured along axes in different directions, such as those produced when light impinges on the orderly array of atoms in a crystalline lattice.

annotation. The ability to attach alphanumeric or other data to a graphics image in a computer.

annotation text. Text that is always displayed in a predetermined size and orientation. See *structure text*.

anomalous dimension. A dimension between normal integer dimensions. For example, a line that wanders around to fill almost all of space intuitively appears to have a dimension greater that 1 (which is the normal dimension of a straight line) and less than 2 (which is the normal dimension of a plane). See *Hausdorff dimension* for an example of how an *anomalous dimension* is found mathematically.

ANSI.   American National Standards Institute. A nongovernment organization which develops and publishes industry-wide standards for voluntary use throughout the United States. Located at 1430 Broadway, New York, NY 10018. Phone 212-642-4900.

ANSI standards.   Standards produced by the American National Standards Institute.

antialiasing or **anti-aliasing.**   1. The act of taking special precautions to limit or eliminate aliasing artifacts. 2. In image generation, any technique that is used to remove the artifacts such as staircasing and line breakup that are caused when producing an image by sampling a picture which has higher spatial frequencies than the sampling frequency. When applied to individual primitives rather than the whole image, other artifacts may be introduced. Techniques that are applied before sampling actually prevent aliasing rather than remove it. There are several commonly used filters for antialiasing. The *box filter* simply picks the closest values for interpolation. The *Gaussian filter* makes use of the Gaussian function for weighting. The Gaussian function is

$$Gaussian_{\frac{1}{\sqrt{n}}}(x) = 2^{-nx^2}$$

The most commonly used values of n are 2 and 4. The *Lanczos2 sinc filter* uses the Lanczos2 sinc function for weighting. This function is

$$Lanczos2(x) = \begin{cases} \dfrac{\sin(\pi x)}{\pi x} \dfrac{\sin(\pi\frac{x}{2})}{\pi\frac{x}{2}}, & |x| < 2 \\ 0, & |x| \geq 2 \end{cases}$$

antialiasing, analytic.   The use of mathematical techniques to determine directly the exact solutions needed to perform antialiasing (within the limits of computer precision).

antialiasing, numerical.   Use of numerical techniques to obtain estimates for the information needed to perform anti-aliasing.

anti-halation backing.   A coating on the back surface of a film that absorbs light and thereby prevents reflection back to the film emulsion, which would cause a *halo* or glowing effect that reduces resolution.

antipersistence. The quality of not having independent increments.

A-O. Acousto-Optic. Method of using sound waves passing through a transparent medium to deflect a beam of laser light.

APA. All points addressable. An array in which every cell can be individually addressed.

aperiodic orbit. An orbit in which the same value never occurs twice.

aperiodic tiling. Filling of a plane by two different tiles.

aperiodicity. Irregularly occurring; not having a period.

aperture. The light-admitting area of a camera lens, or the light-admitting area defined by an adjustable diagram used with the camera lens. Together, the aperture and lens focal length determine the depth of field of the lens.

apfelmannchen. German for *apple mannikin*. A name applied to the Mandelbrot set in many German-originated publications. The set is a plot representing the result of iterating the equation

$$z_{n+1} = z_n^2 + c$$

where z and c are both complex numbers. For a picture of this set, see *Mandelbrot set*.

API. Application programmer's interface. Those portions of a program which create the look and feel of a program interface and determine how it is used.

Apollonian packing of circles. A fractal produced by drawing three circles tangent to each other, then filling the circular triangle created by the three circles with the largest circle tangent to all three, which creates three smaller circular triangles, each of which is filled with the largest circle tangent to the three bounding circles, and continuing the process forever. The resulting figure is also known as the *Apollonian gasket* or *Apollonian net*.

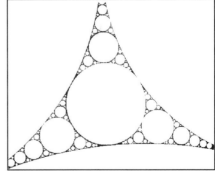

Apollonian Packing of Circles

apostlib. An international unit of luminance. An *apostlib* is equal to 0.1 millilambert. Also known as a *blondel*.

apparent length. The length an object appears to have to an observer as opposed to its true length.

Apple computer. Apple Computer Co. was founded in 1976 by Steve Jobs and Steve Wozniak, who designed the Apple 1, a simple personal computer based on the 6502 microprocessor chip. Apple has grown to be one of the largest personal computer companies. Its current Macintosh models are well known for their desktop publishing and graphics capabilities.

application program. A software program designed to accomplish some particular set of tasks unrelated to computer systems operation, as opposed to a *system program* whose primary purpose is to improve computer operations.

application programmer's interface. Those portions of a program which create the look and feel of a program interface and determine how it is used.

applications binary interface. Low-level interface specifications for a graphics or software system.

approximating fraction.   When a continued fraction is used to represent the true value of a fraction, an *approximating fraction* is created by breaking off the continued fraction at any point. The more terms included in the approximating fraction, the closer the approximation approaches the true value.

approximating function. A continued fraction used to approximate a function.

approximation. A simplified expression which gives an estimate of the true value of a function.

APT. Automatically programmed tool. A programming language for describing the motions of tools required to perform particular machining operations using digitally controlled machining equipment.

arbitration. A protocol used to determine which of competing modules requesting use of a computer bus shall be given control.

arc. 1. A portion of a circle or ellipse. 2. In typeface design, a curved stroke that is a part of a character not enclosing an area.

Archimedean solids, semi-regular. A solid whose faces are regular n-gons with more than one n in symmetric arrangement.

Archimedean spiral. A spiral curve generated by the equations

$$x = r_x \theta \cos(\theta)$$
$$y = r_y \theta \sin(\theta)$$

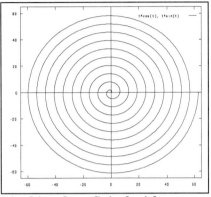

Archimedean Spiral with $r_x = r_y$.

Archimedes cup. A solid constructed by expanding a parabola into the third dimension by dividing it into successively smaller triangular shapes and applying a negative midpoint displacement in altitude to each side of each triangular shape.

architecture. 1. The style of design of a computer system at the functional module level so as to create a machine that is simple and logical. 2. The style of the microprocessor chip used as the basis for a computer such as 80386 architecture or 6880 architecture.

archiving. Storing a backup copy of digital data for future reference, particularly if the working copy is somehow destroyed. With DOS systems, it is possible to mark working files as having been archived so that a subsequent back-up only needs to consider those files that are new or have been changed.

arcsine law. The arcsine law says that the probability $p_{2n}(2k)$ that a random walking particle will spend $2k$ time units in a positive region in the time interval from 0 to $2n$ is given by

$$p_{2n}(2k) = \binom{2k}{k}\binom{2n-2k}{n-k} 2^{-2n}$$

area block. One of a number of equally sized regions of terrain features that comprise a terrain data base for flight simulation graphics.

area filling. Any method for filling a closed two-dimensional figure with a given color. Many graphics programs have built-in software for filling circles, arcs, and polygons. Another form of filling is *flood-filling*, where a seed point is selected within a bounded surface and color fill proceeds in all directions from this point until the boundaries are encountered.

area-filling curve. An infinitely long curve that will completely fill a plane.

area-length relation for river basins. Relationship between the length of a river and the area of its drainage basin, which demonstrates the fractal nature of a river's curve. The relationship is

$$K = \frac{(river\ G\text{-}length)^{0.6}}{(basin\ G\text{-}area)}$$

where *river G-length* is the river's length measured with a ruler of length *G* and *basin G-area* is the area of the river basin measured with the same *G* ruler.

area-number relation for islands. An empirical law which gives the number of islands of a region that are above a given area. The expression is

$$Nr(A{>}a) = F'a^{-B}$$

where $Nr(A{>}a)$ is the number of islands whose area is greater than a and F' and B are positive constants, with B being less than ½.

arithmetic instruction. An assembly language instruction which causes the processor to perform an arithmetic operation (such as add, subtract, compare, increment, or negate).

arithmetic mean. A number that is inserted between two other numbers in an arithmetic progression having a value such that the formula $l = a + (n - 1)d$ (where a is the first term, l is the nth term, n is the number of terms, and d is the common difference) is preserved.

Arnold tongues. Frequency-locked regions of a Cantor set fractal.

Arnold's cat map. A two-dimensional map for the description of Hamiltonian nonlinear systems based on the equations

$$x_{n+1} = x_n + y_n \bmod 1$$

$$y_{n+1} = x_n + 2y_n \bmod 1$$

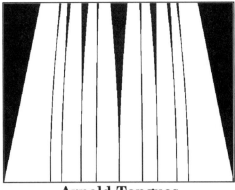

Arnold Tongues

The expression *mod 1* means that only fractions in the half-open unit interval [0, 1] are considered.

ARPANET. Advanced Research Project Agency Network. A pioneering computer network that linked computers of colleges, universities, government agencies, nonprofit laboratories, and industry. Developed and managed by the Advanced Research Project Agency of the U. S. Department of Defense. *ARPANET* developed into the currently used Internet.

Arnold's Cat Map

arrowhead. Another name for the Sierpinski fractal triangle. This curve can be created by starting with a filled-in equilateral triangle and removing the triangle created by connecting the midpoints of the sides. This leaves four filled-in equilateral triangles for which the same process is repeated, and the procedure then continues for as long as desired. The curve is interesting because it turns out that if the proper parameters are inserted in a lot of different fractal generating methods, the result is a Sierpinski triangle. See *Sierpinski triangle* for a picture of this fractal.

articulated figure. A computer representation, usually of the human figure, in which the arms, legs, etc., are capable of being moved with respect to one another.

articulated object. A computer graphics construction that has various parts which move with respect to one another.

artifact. A visible difference between a computer image and the real visual image, usually due to limitations of the computer graphics rather than software mistakes.

artifacts, dithering. Unwanted patterns that are superimposed on an image as a result of dithering.

artificial intelligence. The representation of human thinking activities by machines. The goal is a computer program that reasons in a way similar to that of human beings, but, while computers are better than humans at storing and remembering data, there are many intuitive mechanisms in human reasoning that we currently cannot understand and cannot reproduce. For example, a chess master often looks ten moves ahead to assess the consequences of the currently proposed move. Even the fastest computer would take years to evaluate all the possibilities. Obviously the chess master does some sort of selection process to reduce the number of possibilities that he or she assesses, but we haven't yet determined the criteria that he or she uses.

artificial object. A member of the catalog of graphics objects in a flight simulation environment which is used for convenience of computer operations but is not actually displayed.

artificial reality. A computer simulation of the world which provides video and audio inputs and permits the user to manually interact with the display so that the simulation seems to be the same as actuality. See *virtual reality*.

Arzela–Ascoli theorem. A theorem of rational mapping that states that a family F is normal on D if and only if it is equicontinuous there.

ascent line. A horizontal line corresponding to the maximum height of any character in a type font.

ASCII. American Standard Code for Information Exchange. A standard for encoding alphanumerics and control characters into 7-bit binary code.

ASCII sort. Sorting of a list of data according to the ASCII code.

ASIC. Application Specific Integrated Circuit. A proprietary integrated circuit design produced through standardized methods of modifying standard integrated circuit cell assemblies or gate arrays.

aspect. A property of a graphics primitive (color, for example) which does not affect its geometry.

aspect ratio. The ratio of width to height of a graphics entity such as a pixel, a character block, or the entire graphics display. Computer monitors and television sets have an aspect ratio of 4:3.

assert. To set the level of an electronic control signal to the state in which the control action is initiated.

Association for Computing Machinery. Society for those involved professionally with computer hardware or software. Located at 1515 Broadway, New York, NY 10036.

asymptotic self-similarity. A sequence that is only self-similar as the number of recursions approaches infinity. As an example, consider the following equation based on the infinite product for $2/\pi$

$$s_n = \prod_{k=1}^{n} f_k - \frac{2}{\pi}$$

which has the recursion

$$f_{k+1} = \left(\frac{1+f_k}{2}\right)^{\frac{1}{2}} \qquad f_0 = 0$$

For $n = 1, 2, 3, 4, \ldots$ the solutions to the equation are

$s_1 = 0.070482$
$s_2 = 0.016620$
$s_3 = 0.004109$
$s_4 = 0.0001024$

These terms approach a constant scaling factor of 4.0, so that the expression is self-similar only in the limit as $n \rightarrow \infty$. Thus the expression is *asymptotically self-similar*.

asymptotic value. The value of a line that is associated with a curve such that as a point moves along an infinite branch of the curve the slope of the curve approaches the slope of the line and the distance between the point on the curve and the nearest point on the line approaches zero.

AT. Advanced Technology. A model of the IBM Personal Computer using an Intel 80286 microprocessor and a 16-bit I/O bus. Often applied to similar IBM-compatible 80286 computers.

atmosphere. Computer graphics modeling of visual effects produced by the earth's atmosphere such as fog, clouds, haze, smog, and light attenuation.

atom. 1. The smallest particle of a chemical element. 2. The smallest amount of work that must be processed by a computer without interruption.

atomic. 1. Compact software module containing all necessary elements for a particular task. 2. Computer processor state that can be updated by a single (uninterruptible) instruction.

atomic unit of length. A measure of length corresponding to the radius of a hydrogen atom. It is 5.3×10^{-11} meters.

attenuation. Decrease of wave energy due to absorption by the medium of propagation, such as sound or light falloff with travel through the atmosphere.

attraction, basin of. The area of a strange attractor that includes all points which, upon iteration of the attractor's iterated equation, approach a particular point. Same as *domain of attraction*.

attractive cycle. A cycle of period n is an *attractive cycle* of f if it contains an attractive periodic point of f having the period n.

attractive periodic orbit. A periodic orbit for which the absolute value of its eigenvalue is greater than zero and less than one.

attractor. A set of points to which a number of nearby orbits converge upon repeated iteration.

attractor, Henon. The attractor produced by the recursive formulas

$$x_{n+1} = y_n - a*x_n^2 + 1$$

$$y_{n+1} = b*x_n$$

attractor, Lorenz. The attractor produced as the solution to the dynamical set of equations

$$x' = a*(y - x)$$
$$y' = b*x - y - x*z$$
$$z' = x*y - c*z$$

attractor, parabola. The attractor produced by repeated iteration of the recursive formula

$$p_{n+1} = p_n + k*p_n*(1-p_n)$$

attractor, Rossler. The attractor produced by repeated iteration of the recursive formulas

$$x' = -(y + z)$$
$$y' = x + (\frac{y}{5})$$
$$z' = \frac{1}{5} + z*(x - 5.7)$$

attractor, strange. A set of values on which many orbits of a dynamical set of equations tend to land.

attractor, Verhulst. The attractor produced by repeated iteration of the formula

$$p_{n+1} = p_n + \frac{1}{2}*k*(3*p_n*(1 - p_n) - p_{n-1}*(1 - p_{n-1}))$$

attribute. A property of a graphics primitive not directly associated with its underlying geometry. Some typical properties are color shade and intensity, line width, and area pattern.

attribute controller. Registers in a VGA card which contribute to the translation of 4-bit codes from display memory into 6-bit color register assignments.

AutoCAD. A computer program for creating complex mechanical drawings. Available from Autodesk Retail Products, 11911 North Creek Parkway South, Bothell, WA 98011.

autoconfiguration. A software technique which enables a computer to identify the configuration of a hardware system and adjust its operations accordingly.

autocorrelation function. The mathematical function

$$c(\tau) = \int u(t)u^*(t+\tau)dt$$

which is the correlation of a signal with its delayed self. A waveform needs to be designed so that its *autocorrelation function* has values as near zero as possible except when $\tau = 0$ if resolution of data is needed. Applying the *autocorrelation function* can then reduce noise effects and extract signals otherwise buried in noise.

autodimensioning. A feature of CAD and drafting programs that automatically computes the (scaled) distance between two points, draws dimension lines, and inserts the proper numerical value.

Autofact. Conference held in Detroit or Chicago annually each November. It is concerned with design tools applied to the automobile industry. Currently many of these tools are graphics oriented. The conference is sponsored by the Society of Manufacturing Engineers.

automatic display detection. A feature of some VGA cards, in which the card automatically detects the type of monitor connected to it and reconfigures itself for proper interface.

automatic size adjustment. A feature of some VGA cards in which signals to the monitor are automatically adjusted so that displays of different resolutions and numbers of pixels all fill the entire display screen.

autosense. A capability built into some display adapter cards that have the ability to use either an 8- or 16-bit bus interface. *Autosense* detects whether the interface bus is 8 or 16 bits and automatically selects the proper hardware and software configuration to work with the detected bus.

AutoShade. A program for drawing realistic pictures using the personal computer.

autosizing. Capability of a display adapter to adjust size automatically so that displays of different resolutions and numbers of pixels fill the entire screen.

A/UX. A variation of the UNIX operating system designed to be run on Apple Macintosh computers.

auxiliary video extension. A connector on an EGA or VGA card which provides video signals for an unspecified purpose. These connectors still exist on many cards, but are seldom used.

average contractivity condition. The case where repetition of a set of affine transformations always results in convergence.

AVS. Application visualization system. A high-level graphic software interface developed by Stellar Computer, Inc.

axial ray. The ray that is the center of a bundle of rays.

axiom. In mathematics, a statement of self-evident truth.

axis. 1. Any lengthwise central line around which parts of a body are centrally arranged. 2. One of the three mutually perpendicular lines (x, y, and z) which make up the cartesian coordinate system. The location of any point in cartesian three-dimensional space is referenced to these axes.

axis of symmetry. A real or imaginary center line around which parts of a body are symmetrically arranged.

azimuthal equal-area projection. A mapping of a sphere onto a plane that employs a simple scale change to account for the area contributions as the radius changes incrementally from the chart center.

azimuthal equidistant projection. A mapping of a sphere onto a plane that gives simultaneous bearing and radial distance for great-circle travel away from the chart center.

B

back clipping plane. A plane perpendicular to the line of sight, beyond which all objects are clipped, or removed from the image. The *yon* plane.

back porch. The portion of a composite television signal which includes the part of the blanking pulse that contains the color burst signal.

back up. v. To make a copy of a program or data set for use in case the primary program or data set fails.

backbone. 1. The part of a communications network which carries the heaviest traffic. 2. The part of a network which joins local area networks (LANs) together.

backface culling. The process of testing faces of a convex polygon object and eliminating those that are not visible (as identified by the fact that the normal to the face is pointed away from the screen) so that they do not have to be processed for display.

backfacing. A polygon in an image being rendered that has its normal pointing away from the current observer viewpoint. A backfacing polygon is not included in the image view and therefore can be eliminated from further processing.

background. 1. In image processing, a default image used when a ray intercepts no other graphics primitive object. 2. The execution of one or more programs simultaneously with the execution of a main program which is using the display screen.

background color. 1. The default color to which every pixel in an image window is initialized. 2. The color used to display pixels which are not changed by a series of graphics operations.

background ink. A reflective ink used on parts of a document that are not supposed to be picked up by an optical scanner.

backing store. Portions of an image that are stored when they are covered by a window so that they may be restored when the window is removed.

backlit. A display screen that has a light source behind the image to enhance viewing under low ambient light conditions. A cathode-ray tube screen does not need to be backlit, since the data are florescent and therefore are lighted when there is no ambient light at all. However, LCD displays cannot be seen at all unless they are backlit or there is good ambient lighting.

backplane. A circuit board providing power and communications wiring and connectors for daughter circuit boards.

backup. n. A copy of programs or data that is kept in a safe location for use in restoring the primary program or data if it fails, as for example, when a hard disk crashes. When a disk failure or other similar catastrophe occurs, only data inserted since the last backup was made are lost. If no backup exists, all data are lost. Before a backup copy is used to restore a failed data set, one should make sure that the condition that caused the original failure will not also destroy the backup.

backwards ray tracing. The generation of a scene by tracing rays of light from the observer viewpoint to each pixel on the viewing screen and thence to objects in the scene that are intercepted by the ray. From the first object encountered rays are traced according to how they are reflected or refracted by the object.

bad sector. A defective segment of a floppy disk or hard disk. Bad sectors are often present from the beginning as a result of disk manufacturing defects. Such sectors are automatically locked out by the disk formatting program. A sector that goes bad after having part of a program or data written to it usually makes it impossible to recover the lost information. If errors occur in a sector, operating systems usually try several rereads and also sometimes use error correcting techniques before giving up and admitting that the sector is bad.

ballistic gain. A feature of some trackballs and mice that makes the cursor move faster when the user moves the mouse or trackball faster.

balloon help. A feature of the Macintosh System 7, in which on-screen help instructions are shown in balloons similar to dialog in a cartoon.

banding. An artifact of using normal coding to store image information. It manifests itself as bands of color across a single colored object.

bandwidth. The frequency range over which a bus, interface, or device is capable of transferring digital information.

bar chart. A graph in which data values are represented by the lengths of rectangles.

bar code. A system of vertical lines of variable width which are converted to alphanumeric data by a scanning device. The *UPC* code used for supermarket pricing is an example.

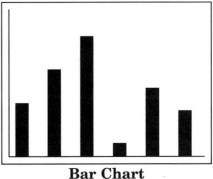

Bar Chart

bare winding number. The frequency ratio of a circle map.

barrel distortion. A defect of display systems in which sides of a rectangle bulge outward to look like the outline of a barrel.

base alignment. The arrangement of columns of text so that the text is aligned across the entire page regardless of the size of elements in each of the columns.

base font. The typeface that is used by default when no other typeface is specified.

baseline. An imaginary line upon which characters of a type font appear to rest. Individual characters may have descenders that drop below the baseline.

basic matrix. A matrix that provides information on how to interpret a geometric matrix of control points in order to generate a bicubic patch.

basin boundary metamorphoses. A sudden jump in the boundary of a basin of attraction as a parameter is changed.

basin of attraction. The area of a strange attractor that includes all points which upon iteration of the attractor's iterated equation approach a particular point. Same as *domain of attraction*.

basis spline. See *B-spline*.

basis weight. A measurement of the weight (and therefore quality) of paper. This is given as the weight of 500 sheets (one ream) of 24 inch × 36 inch sheets. Common letterhead paper weights are in the range of 20 to 24 pounds.

batch processing. The processing of a group of computer programs in a single operation.

baud rate. Rate of serial data transmission (from J. E. Baudot, inventor of serial code for telegraphy). The *baud rate* is the reciprocal of the duration in seconds of the shortest signal element. In normal computer serial data transfer, this corresponds to the transmission rate in bits per second.

Bayer dithering. A method of dithering in which each 8 × 8 block of pixels in a source image is compared with a fixed 8 × 8. Pixels larger than the corresponding pattern pixel are colored white. The remaining pixels are colored black.

BCC. Block check character. A control character appended to a block of data which is used to determine whether the received block contains errors. See *CRC*.

beam penetration display. A type of color cathode-ray tube in which layers of red and green phosphors are applied to the interior of the faceplate in such a way that the color of the display depends upon the amount that the electron beam penetrates the phosphor layers, which in turn depends upon the electron beam accelerating voltage. It provides simpler and higher resolution displays than color-mask tubes, but cannot produce shades of blue. Also known as a *penetron*.

beam recording. A method of recording directly on film using a laser or electron beam.

beam tracing. A method of ray tracing in which intersection computations are made for a polygonal cone of rays rather than a single ray, in order to minimize computations due to the coherence of adjacent rays.

bed of nails. A fixture having many pin-type probes that impinge on various points of a printed circuit board to permit internal testing of the board.

benchmark. A set of computer software that exercises a wide variety of computer functions. A *benchmark* is used to test various computers and computer configurations and obtain comparisons of time and performance characteristics.

BER. Bit error rate. A measurement of the average number of errors that occur during data transmission.

Bernoulli box. A hard disk storage system with removable disks that uses the Bernoulli principle of fluid dynamics discovered by the 18th-century Swiss scientist Daniel Bernoulli. This technique makes use of the high-speed revolution of the hard disk to create an air cushion that keeps the read/write head at the desired distance from the disk's surface, thereby avoiding any frictional wear effects between the disk and the head.

Bernstein basis function. A polynomial used to compute a Bezier curve. Also known as a *Bernstein polynomial*.

beta spline. A method of curve drawing used for graphics modeling. The *beta spline* is a derivation of the generalized uniform cubic B-spline.

beta test. Testing of a new software product by actual users prior to its release as a commercial product. Extensive beta testing uncovers many problems that are not discovered during testing by the software manufacturer and thus produces a more robust final product.

Bethe lattice. A graph without loops in which each node has the same number of branches. Also known as a *Cayley tree*.

beveling. Filling in to permit joining of two wide lines whose end center points are coincident.

bezel. The metal or plastic frame that surrounds a display or dial.

Bezier curve. A type of curve that is defined as the function-weighted sum of four or more control points, two at the ends of the curve and two other points. A *Bezier curve* always lies within the convex hull of its control points.

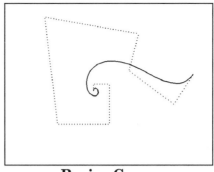

Bezier patch. A type of bicubic patch formed by using Bezier curves.

Bezier Curve

Bezier simplices. Surfaces such as triangles, tetrahedra, and so forth, whose sides are Bezier curves.

BFT. Binary file transmission. A standard for transmitting facsimile data between two fax boards that is faster than conventional fax transmission techniques.

bicubic patch. A small piece used to define part of an arbitrary surface. It is defined by three polynomials of third degree with respect to parameters s and t.

bidirectional printing. A technique for increasing a printer's speed by printing a line from left to right, the next line from right to left, the next line from left to right, etc., in contrast to unidirectional printing where every line is printed from left to right.

bidirectional reflectance. A function applied over a small solid angle to relate incoming light intensity in a given direction to outgoing light intensity in another direction.

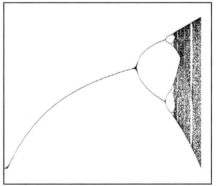

bifurcate. To divide in two.

bifurcation diagram. A fractal picture that shows where an iterated equation splits into two or more solutions and where areas of chaos occur.

Bifurcation Diagram

bilevel. A monochrome display technique in which each pixel is assigned one of two levels, either black or white.

bilinear interpolation. Interpolation to obtain the value of a point located within a triangle or quadrilateral by a series of linear interpolations between the vertices of the triangle or quadrilateral.

bilinear patch. A quadrilateral in three-dimensional space defined by four vertices that need not be coplanar. Intermediate points on the patch are determined by linear interpolation from the vertices.

binary decomposition. A method of creating fractal curves of Julia sets.

binary file transmission. (BFT). A standard for transmitting facsimile data between two fax boards that is faster than conventional fax transmission techniques.

binary order, animation recording. A method of recording animation frames in which halfway through the recording process, the animation is double-framed, one-quarter through the process, the animation is quadruple-framed, one-eighth through the process, the animation is octuple-framed, and so forth. This permits animation errors to be detected earlier than they would if sequential recording were used.

binary recursive subdivision. A technique for determining the intersection between a ray and a triangle.

binary search method. A technique for searching that depends upon representing the datum searched for as a binary number. The data to be searched are divided into two bins, those whose most significant binary digit is one and those whose most significant binary digit is zero. The bin containing the desired datum is then divided again based on the next most significant binary digit, and this process is repeated until only the desired datum remains.

binary space partition tree. (BSP tree). A technique for subdividing three-dimensional space with planes so that each resulting partition contains the same number of primitive objects. Reduces the number of computations required for intersection computation or hidden surface removal. Also known as a *Btree* or *binary tree*.

binding. 1. In networking, the process whereby a network station connects itself to a server to obtain desired services. 2. The attachment of more generally defined programs and parameters to a specific computer language.

binocular disparity. The difference in perspective between the views from the two eyes of an observer due to the fact that each eye is located at a different position.

bis. Term used by CCITT to designate the second in a family of related standards. The term *ter* designates the third in the family.

bisection, Sturm sequences. A method used to isolate any real root of $f(x) = 0$. It starts with an interval

$$b > a; \ s(a) - s(\infty) \geq k; \ s(b) - s(\infty) < k$$

Repeated bisection of the interval will isolate the root to any desired accuracy.

bit. Contraction of binary digit. The smallest unit of data, a bit may have either of two conditions: on or off, or 1 or 0.

bit error rate. (BER). A measurement of the average number of errors that occur during data transmission.

bit-map. A representation of characters or graphics in a display by individual pixels usually arranged in order of a row of pixels horizontally and then additional similar rows to make up all the rows in the display. Monochrome data can be represented by one bit per pixel. Color displays may require up to 32 bits per pixel, which may be sequential or a separate *bit-map* may be generated for each bit of the color representation.

bit-map rotator. A routine that rotates a bit-map using table look-up.

bit-mapped font. A set of bit patterns that represents all of the characters of a type font of a particular size.

bit-mapped graphics. Images that are drawn on a display by a raster scan which scans from left to right in rows and then from top to bottom, with each dot that is to make up the image illuminated at the proper point in the scan.

bit plane. A memory buffer that holds one bit which is partial definition of pixel color. Thus, to define 16 colors, one might use four bit planes. Combining the bit values from each of the four planes for the same pixel address at each plane would yield the 4-bit color information for the addressed pixel.

bit plane encoding. Application of run-length encoding to each bit plane separately to compress and store an image.

bit specifications. The number of colors or gray levels that may be displayed at one time. This depends upon the characteristics of the graphics controller card and the amount of memory it contains. The EGA can display 4-bit color, for a total of 16 colors. The VGA can display 8-bit color for a total of 256 colors. Super VGA cards may have 16-bit color (65,536 total colors) or 24-bit color (16.8 million colors).

bitblt. Bit block transfer. A technique for fast movement of a (usually rectangular) collection of bits to/from or in display memory. Used to display moving objects.

bits per inch. (bpi). The number of bits stored per linear inch on a magnetic tape.

bits per second. (bps). The number of bits transferred in a data communications system in one second.

black level. The voltage level of the displayable part of a video signal which corresponds to a completely black video input.

black line. A positive image, wherein the images consist of black lines on a white background.

black matrix. A picture tube in which each group of color phosphor dots is surrounded by black for increased contrast and clarity.

black noise. Noise that has a power spectrum proportional to f^β where $\beta > 2$.

blackbody. An idealized object that emits all of the light produced by the body at a specified temperature.

blanking. The process of shutting off the electron beam of a cathode-ray tube between sweeps so that nothing is shown on the screen while the deflection circuits reposition themselves for the next horizontal or vertical sweep.

blanking level. The voltage level of a video signal that totally suppresses the electron beam of the cathode-ray tube during blanking. Also knows as *pedestal level*.

bleed. In publishing, the positioning of a picture on a page in such a way that it extends beyond the margin to the very edge of the page. Normally such a picture extends slightly beyond the finished dimension of the page, with the excess trimmed off during binding.

bleeding. 1. In a cathode-ray tube display, a phenomena in which the color of one pixel affects the color of neighboring pixels.   2. The appearance of colored light on a surface that is produced by diffuse reflection from another surface. This makes the surface appear to be different from its true color. For example, a blue carpet can bleed a light blue tinge to nearby white walls.

bleeding white. A defect in display systems which results in white areas appearing to flow into black areas.

blend surface. A surface added to provide continuous transition between two intersecting surfaces in a graphics model.

blending. The transitioning of one line, surface or color into another smoothly without an observable joining edge.

blending functions. The weights that are applied to two curves to assure continuity without an observable junction. They are usually in the form of cubic polynomials.

blinking. Changing the intensity or color of a particular graphics area in order to highlight it.

blip. 1. A target signal on a radar screen. 2. A timing or counting mark placed on a microfilm.

blob. An algebraic surface that can be defined by a quadratic equation. A number of blobs can be combined to approximate an irregular surface in a way that simplifies ray tracing.

block. Quantity of data recorded on a disk or magnetic tape in a single continuous operation. Blocks are identified by track and sector addresses and are separated by physical gaps.

block check character. (BCC). A control character appended to a block of data which is used to determine whether the received block contains errors. See *CRC*.

blondel. A unit of luminance equal to 0.1 millilambert.

blooming. A condition in a video display or video camera in which excessive brightness causes white areas to expand and cover up darker areas.

blue noise. A set of samples having a frequency distribution which is close to that of a Poisson distribution.

body color model. Software that models the absorption of light through a translucent media.

boilerplate. Text material that is used over and over again without change in different documents.

Bolanzo-Weierstrass theorem. A theorem that states that every infinite sequence x_n, where n is an integer between 1 and infinity, of S contains a subsequence which is a Cauchy sequence.

boot. To start up a computer. Usually, permanently built-in software causes the computer to read a designated sector or sectors from a disk. These sectors, in turn, give instructions from which the computer loads the entire operating system.

Borel field. If (X, d) is a metric space and $\mathcal{B}$ is the σ-field generated by the open subsets of X, then $\mathcal{B}$ is called the *Borel field* associated with the metric space. Any element of $\mathcal{B}$ is called a *Borel subset* of X.

bounce light. Synonym for bleeding.

boundary representation. (B-rep). Specifying the surfaces of an object in order to model it, as contrasted to defining an object by the intersection of primitive solids as in constructive solid geometry.

boundary scanning method. A method of generating fractal curves from Julia sets.

bounding box. A rectangular polyhedron that encompasses one or more primitive objects. Used to simplify ray tracing. If a ray doesn't intersect the bounding box, one knows that it doesn't intersect the enclosed primitive objects, so no more testing is required. Only if the ray intersects the bounding box is it necessary to perform more complex tests to see if the ray intersects one of the enclosed objects. This reduces the amount of computer time required for intersect testing.

bounding sphere. Similar to a bounding box, except that the bounding solid is a sphere.

bounding volume. Similar to a bounding box, except that instead of a rectangular polyhedron, any shaped solid that permits easy intersect testing may be used.

bounding volume for torus. A volume that consists of a sphere cut by two planes, which encloses a torus. It is the most efficient bounding volume for determining intersection of a ray with a torus.

box filter. A method for modifying the color value of a pixel by averaging it with the color values of those pixels surrounding it. Used in anti-aliasing.

bpi. Bits per inch. The number of bits stored per linear inch on a magnetic tape.

bps. Bits per second. The number of bits transferred in a data communications system in one second.

branch. One of two or more lines, curves, or solid objects that meet at a node.

branch plane. The plane that contains a branch.

break action. 1. A set of predetermined instructions that directs a COM system about where to place the next block of data after a break condition. 2. Indication of the end of a recorded frame of data in a COM system.

Brent's method. A technique for inversion of monotonic functions in a single variable.

B-rep. Boundary representation. Specifying the surfaces of an object in order to model it, as contrasted to defining an object by the intersection of primitive solids as in constructive solid geometry.

Bresenham's algorithm. A mathematical algorithm for determining which pixels should be illuminated for the most accurate representation of a straight line, given a specified pixel resolution.

Bresenham's circle algorithm. A variation of Bresenham's algorithm that draws a circle rather than a straight line.

brightness. 1. The average light intensity of an image. 2. The perceived amount of light as determined by the luminance and chrominance of the source. Brightness is based upon the perception of the human eye, which varies with frequency, so that brightness is not proportional to physical energy emitted.

brilliant. Having both a high color value and a high degree of color saturation.

brown noise. Noise that has a power spectrum proportional to f^2.

Brownian motion. A path that is defined as the integral of white noise.

B-spline. Basis spline. A method of specifying control points to determine the shape of a curve that is very similar to the Bezier curve, but permits additional control of shape and continuity.

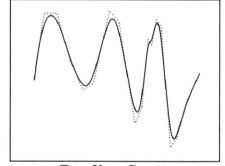

B-spline patch. A bicubic patch formed using B-spline curves.

B-spline Curve

BSP tree. Binary space partition tree. A technique for subdividing three-dimensional space with planes so that each resulting partition contains the same number of primitive objects. Reduces the number of computations required for intersection computation or hidden surface removal.

Btree. See *BSP tree*.

bubble. A technique for recording data on optical disks in which a laser beam strikes nonimage areas, causing bubbles to form, while the image area remains clear to reflect the light of the reading laser.

bubble sort. A technique for sorting lists of words into alphabetical or numerical order. The *bubble sort* scans a list until it finds a number or letter that is lower than the first number or letter in the list and then exchanges the two. It then picks up where it left off on the list and continues making comparisons with the first number. When the list has been completely scanned, the process is repeated, starting and comparing with the second number or letter, and so forth until finally everything is compared with the next to last number. At that point, the list is completely sorted.

bubble test. A form of clipping in which a computed sphere surrounding a portion of a three-dimensional graphics volume is used as the clipping boundary.

buffer. Memory space designed for temporary storage. Usually used when data arrive from a transmitting device at a rate faster than they can be accepted by the receiving device.

bug. A defect in computer hardware or software.

bug list. A list of known defects in a particular version of a piece of computer software together with suggestions for getting around the problems until a new edition of the software is released.

bump mapping. Producing the appearance of a nonsmooth surface on an object by randomly perturbing the direction of the surface normal prior to computing the shading for each pixel.

bundle table. A table of workstation-dependent aspects for a particular primitive in the GKS or PHIGS graphics standards.

Burkes error diffusion filter. A dithering technique in which the error between the color of a pixel and its representation by black or white is partially added to the two pixels on the right of the current pixel as well as the five pixels surrounding the current pixel location on the line below.

burst. See *color burst*.

bus. A set of lines on which signals are entered for use by many connected devices.

bus mouse. A mouse that is connected to a computer through an expansion card slot rather than through a serial port.

butterfly effect. The image generated by plotting the solutions of the Lorenz strange attractor equations. See *attractor, Lorenz*.

button. 1. A mechanical switch-like device, as on a mouse, which provides an input to a computer. 2. An image on a display that gives the appearance of a mechanical button. It is activated by using a mouse to position the cursor on the button image and then activating the mouse mechanical button.

Butz's algorithm. An algorithm for generating an n-dimensional Peano curve.

byte. A unit of computer data consisting of eight bits.

C

C. A computer language originated by D. Ritche and used to write the UNIX operating system. C provides the most flexibility of any computer language at the price of not including very many safeguards against programmer misuse of the language. C is the most widely used language for the development of professional programs.

C++. An extension of the C language by Bjarne Stroustrup to include object-oriented programming techniques and the overriding of mathematical operators.

C3 or C^3. Military command, control, and communications systems.

cache. (käsh). A portion of high speed memory used to store frequently used disk data so as to reduce the retrieval time when the data are required. The success of caching schemes depends upon how well the associated software can determine which data should be included in the cache at any given time.

cache coherency. Keeping data values in a cache consistent with the data in the larger memory that the cache mirrors.

CAD. Computer-aided (or -assisted) design (or drafting). Software used to assist a designer or draftsman in creating a design and the drawing for it. Normally the output of a CAD program actually produces a drawing on a printer or plotter.

CAE. Computer-aided engineering. Computer software that simulates hardware designs to permit a device to be analyzed without actually building it.

CAI. Computer-aided instruction. Computer software to facilitate teaching through interactive text, questions, and responses of the computer to correct or incorrect answers.

calligraphic display. A type of cathode-ray tube display in which lines and characters are drawn by directly moving the electron beam to trace out the desired shape rather than scanning the beam in a raster and illuminating the appropriate points in the raster scan. Also known as a *stroke display* or *stroker*.

CAM. Computer-aided (or -assisted) manufacturing. A system which can take the output of a CAD program and use it to directly operate machinery to fabricate the part described in the CAD program data file.

camera space. A coordinate system that has its origin at the observer (or camera) viewpoint and its positive z axis pointed along the direction of view.

candela. A unit of luminous intensity. One candela is the amount of light per unit solid angle from a point source. It is equal to one lumen per steradian.

candidate list. In ray tracing, a list of primitive graphics objects which need to be tested for intersection by a given ray.

canonical fill algorithm. An algorithm for filling a closed polygon with a selected color by starting at a seed point within the polygon and expanding in all directions until the polygon is filled. The *canonical fill algorithm* was developed by Smith in 1979.

Cantor set. A set of numbers that has measure zero. The basis of a number of interesting fractals.

capstan. A driven cylinder that drives a magnetic tape at the proper speed. The capstan is usually affixed to a flywheel, which eliminates speed variations of the driving motor. The capstan has a large area in contact with the tape surface, which assures that the tape moves smoothly.

CAR. Computer-assisted retrieval. A computer system that locates documents stored on paper, microfilm, or microfiche. Such a system usually has complex cross-referencing and search capabilities that permit identification of a particular document when a minimum of information is available.

Cardano's formula. A formula for finding the roots of a cubic equation.

carrier. 1. In communication, the radio-frequency signal upon which data are modulated. 2. In electrostatic printing, a substance that moves and disperses toner without actually toning an image.

cartesian coordinates. The common rectangular coordinate system, consisting of three mutually perpendicular axes (x, y, and z), from which all points in a volume are referenced.

cartesian product. Representation of the color of a pixel as a number that combines the three coordinates of a point in three-dimensional space, using scaling to give optimum representation of all colors.

cartography. The mapping of a sphere onto a plane.

CASE. Computer-aided software engineering. A computer program that permits the computer to generate the details of program code when basic relations are entered into the program.

case sensitive. Capable of differentiating between capital and lowercase letters. To a case-sensitive device, *example* and *EXAMPLE* are two different and totally unrelated words.

cassette. A magnetic tape storage device which includes takeup and supply reels as well as a length of tape. The most commonly used cassettes are the VHS, 8-mm, and Beta video units and the ¼-inch audio unit.

Cassini's divisions. The divisions in the rings of Saturn.

catalog. A listing of files and/or directories that are stored in computer memory or on a disk or tape.

cathode-ray tube. (CRT). A display device used in computers and television sets. The cathode-ray tube consists of an electron gun that projects a beam onto a phosphorescent screen. These are enclosed in a glass envelope, the interior of which is evacuated. The electron beam is focused at the desired spot on the screen by electromagnetic coils mounted external to the tube. The electron beam then excites the phosphor at that point, causing it to emit light.

Catmull-Rom patch. A bicubic patch that is generated using Catmull-Rom splines.

Catmull-Rom spline. A type of spline used in generating graphics curves, in which the curve passes through all of the control points.

Cauchy sequence. If x_n is a sequence of points in a metric space (X, d) and this sequence converges to a point x which is within X, then the sequence is a Cauchy sequence.

caustic. In optics, light focused by reflection from or refraction through a curved object.

CAV. Constant angular velocity. A method of data recording in which the same amount of data is recorded for each revolution of a disk, even though it would be possible to record more data at the outer edge of the disk than at the inner edge of the disk.

Cayley tree. A graph without loops in which each node has the same number of branches. Also known as a *Bethe lattice*.

CBT. Computer-based training. An interactive program which enables the computer to teach a subject. Also referred to as *courseware*.

CCD. Charge-coupled devices. An array of light-sensing semiconductors upon which a lens image is focused to convert the image to electrical impulses. The array provides a high-resolution image on a microchip.

CCITT. Comité Consultatif Internationale de Télégraphique et Téléphonique. An international group that develops standards for telephone and telegraph communications.

CD. Compact disk. A 4-3/4-inch disk upon which digital data are recorded for playback by a laser reader. CDs provide a high-quality method of storing music, since the digital recording technique is immune to noise generated with most other recording techniques. CDs have the capability to store large amounts of computer data, but currently methods of home recording such disks are not available. Reading of data is also slower than for hard magnetic disks.

CD-ROM. Compact disk read-only memory. A storage system for digital computer data using CDs as the storage medium. As of 1993, a CD-ROM disk holds about 600 megabytes of data.

cel.   1. An animation technique in which an image is drawn on transparent material so that successive images may be overlayed to produce a composite picture. 2. A pattern consisting of color and transparency values that is mapped as a texture onto a computer graphics scene. Particularly used for clouds, smoke and haze, and tree foliage.

cell.   The color of a rectangular picture element as defined for GKS and PHIGS graphics standards.

cell array.   An array of cells in the GKS graphics standard that defines the color of a patch of an image.

cellular automata.   A technique for modeling growth. *Cellular automata* are made up of mathematical cells in an array. Each cell changes its value or state according to some specified set of algorithms. The state of each cell is affected by the states of neighboring cells.

center of gravity.   The point in a body about which all points of the body balance each other. For a triangle, this is the intersection of the medians.

central projection.   A projection of a sphere onto a plane where the projection is accomplished through rays that begin at the center of the sphere. Also known as *gnomonic projection*.

Centronics interface.   The standard 36-pin parallel interface which is used to connect printers and other parallel devices to a computer. Normally this 36-pin connector is at the printer end of the cable and a standard 25-pin RMA connector is at the other end. Named for the Centronics Corp., who used them in the first parallel printers.

CEPS.   Color electronics prepress system. A system for electronic pagination and imaging for color printing that is computer controlled, using the Neugebauer equations to calculate color values.

Cesaro curve.   A self-similar fractal curve produced by starting with a line segment, replacing it with two lines that with the original would make a right isoceles triangle, and then repeating this for every newly created line segment as many times as desired.

CGA.   Color Graphics Adapter. A graphics adapter card that interfaces the IBM PC and compatibles to a color monitor using a low-resolution color graphics standard.

CGI. 1. Computer generated imagery. Images generated by a computer for display on a computer monitor. 2. Computer Graphics Interface. An ANSI/ISO currently under development that will be used to establish formats for direct communication of graphics primitives from computers to display devices, printers, and plotters. Also known as *virtual device metafile*.

CGM. Computer Graphics Metafile. A computer graphics standard that permits interchange of vector and bit-mapped graphics between widely differing computers.

chad. Confetti scraps produced by punching a computer-punchedcard or by punching the drive holes in tractor-feed printer paper. If the holes are completely punched so that the chad drops out, the resulting form is called a chadded form. If the chad is left hanging by a thread from the form, the form is called a chadless form.

change matrix. A matrix that specifies the direction and amount of change to a transformation matrix.

channel. A layer of information in a frame buffer. Also known as a *plane*. For example, a frame buffer that stores red, green, and blue pixels in separate layers has three *channels* or *planes*.

chaos. The field of mathematics that studies disorderly behavior of equations and physical phenomena.

chaos band. Regions of chaotic behavior between which a function behaves in a normal orderly manner.

chaos game. The application of integrated function systems (IFS) to create fractal images.

character. A letter of the alphabet, a number, or a punctuation mark. If the ASCII code is used, as with PCs, a character is represented by one byte.

character-based user interface. (CUI). A computer system in which user-typed characters are used to control computer operations.

character cell. A matrix of dots assigned for the display of a character. Typical character cell sizes for the PC are 8×8, 8×14, and 8×16. Each character to be displayed is represented by a unique combination of lighted and dark dots in the character cell.

character device. A printer or other output device which receives data from the computer on a character-by-character basis rather than in blocks of data.

character field. The rectangular region that marks the bounds within which a character may be displayed.

character generator. Hardware used to generate predefined characters for display.

character graphics. A set of predefined characters designed to create simple graphics images. Typically it includes single and double vertical lines and various types of intersections of single and double lines.

character pitch. The number of characters per inch in printed or displayed text. The most common pitches are 10 for *pica* typewriter type and 12 for *elite* typewriter type. Strictly speaking, *character pitch* refers only to the width of the character and the height can be anything, but normally, the height of characters of a given pitch is adjusted to produce a pleasing typeface.

character recognition. Techniques whereby a computer can recognize written or printed text.

character set. Those symbols which are available with a particular type font. In English, the *character set* always includes upper and lowercase alphabetical characters, numbers, and some punctuation marks. Other special characters may be available, the exact variety of special characters being dependent upon which type font is selected.

character terminal. A terminal that can display text only, not graphics.

characters per inch. (cpi). The density of characters per inch on paper or tape. For characters on tape, this is the same as *character pitch*.

charge-coupled devices. (CCD). An array of light-sensing semi-conductors upon which a lens image is focused to convert the image to electrical impulses. The array provides a high-resolution image on a microchip.

check bits.   Additional data bits that are inserted into a data transmission to permit determining whether any transmission errors have occurred. The simplest use of check bits is to assign a check bit to a block of n data bits, with the *check bit* a one if the sum of bits that are one in the block is odd and a zero if the sum of the bits that are one in the block is even.

checksum. A set of bits that gives the sum of bits that are one in a block of transmitted data. When compared with the sum of the received block, the *checksum* should be identical if no transmission errors have occurred.

child. 1. A subset of data that is dependent upon another data set. 2. A node in a hierarchy that is below another node.

child program. A second program that is executed by a currently running program without user intervention.

choice device. In the GKS graphics specification, a logical input consisting of a number that indicates the choice of a predetermined set of alternatives.

Chooser. A Macintosh utility that allows user selection of a peripheral device such as a printer, server, modem, scanner, or network.

chroma. The hue and saturation components of a color, not including its brightness.

chroma control. A control on a monitor that adjusts color saturation.

chromatic aberration. A characteristic of glass in lenses that causes rays of different colors to be bent by different amounts, thereby focusing them at different points.

chromaticity diagram. A plot of the (x,y) portion of xyY color space.

chrominance. The part of a composite color video signal that comprises the hue and saturation information. See also *YIQ*. space

CIE. Commission International de l'Èclairage. An international commission on illumination. It is responsible for developing specifications for color matching systems.

CIELAB. The acroynym for the Commission International de l'Èclairage plus *lightness* plus $a*$ and $b*$ axis labels. A standardized color space which provides equal steps of perceived color change (by the eye) for equal changes in the coordinate values. The space is defined in cylindrical coordinates.

cine-mode. Method of recording data on a film strip so that it can be read when the strip is held vertically.

circle. The locus of all points at a given distance from a center point.

circle of confusion. The circle on a projected image produced by a lens transmitting a point of light. For a perfect lens, this circle should be a point. The larger the circle, the poorer the quality of the lens.

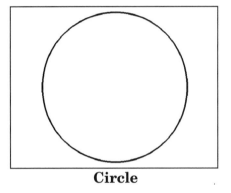

Circle

circular addressing. See *circular buffering.*

circular arc. A portion of the circumference of a circle.

circular buffering. A memory addressing technique in which pointers are stored indicating the beginning and end of the data sequence. Additional data are added to the end and the end pointer changed accordingly. When data are removed, the start pointer is changed to reflect the new beginning of active data. When the end of the buffer area is reached additional data are inserted at the beginning of the buffer area. An error occurs if an attempt is made to store too much data so that data overlap in the buffer.

circumcenter. A point within a triangle that is equidistance from all three vertices.

circumference. The perimeter of a circle.

circumradius. The distance from the circumcenter of a triangle to any of the vertices.

classification.   A ray-tracing technique in which rays are grouped according to direction, origin, or some other characteristic so as to reduce the number of required computations.

clip art.   A collection of digital images from which a user may select pictures for use in his or her own publications.

clip boundary.   The definition of a region outside of which graphics objects are eliminated in producing an image.

clip path.   A two-dimensional boundary outside of which graphics objects are eliminated in producing an image.

clip rectangle.   A rectangular boundary outside of which graphics objects are eliminated in producing an image.

clip region.   In a window system, the portions of the display outside the selected window, from which output is removed by clipping.

clip test.   Any quick test for determining whether a pixel is outside the clip boundary and therefore should not be reproduced.

clipboard.   The temporary memory cache in a Macintosh computer.

clipping.   1. The process of eliminating those portions of graphics primitives that extend beyond a predetermined region, so that they do not appear in a reproduced image. 2. Setting limits to the maximum white and minimum black signals of a composite video signal and eliminating portions of the signal that exceed these limits.

clipping plane.   A plane in three-dimensional space that is parallel to the image plane and which marks the boundary between objects that are to be rendered and those that are not.

closed object.   An object whose surfaces can only be seen from one side, the other side being hidden inside the opaque object.

closure.   The accuracy with which lines that are supposed to meet at a point actually do meet. In mapping, due to surveying, measurement, and scaling errors, there is always an *error of closure*, where two measurements of the same point via different methods give different results. In a final map, these errors are fudged so that the map appears perfectly accurate.

cluster. 1. A group of computers, terminals, or workstations connected in a single system. 2. A group of convex graphics objects that are linearly separable from other such groups so that a plane may be established between two clusters without intersecting either. See *Schumacher algorithm*.

clustered-dot dither. A technique for creating dot patterns similar to those in halftones to permit printing of a photographic image.

CLV. Constant linear velocity. A method of disk drive design in which the disk speed is varied with head position so that the linear amount of disk surface passing under the head in a given time is the same for large outer tracks as it is for smaller inner tracks. This permits more data to be stored on the outer tracks.

C-M interface. The body of information that permits construction of a mathematical model from a conceptual model and the transfer of data between them.

CMYK. Cyan, magenta, yellow, and key (for black). The four subtractive colors used in color printing. All colors in a picture are comprised of these four basic colors. Color printing is accomplished by four passes through the printing press, each pass using ink of one of these basic colors.

coax. Coaxial cable. A cable consisting of an inner conductor surrounded by an insulator and then a sheath of shielding braid. Coaxial cable is designed to have a characteristic impedance so that it can be matched to prevent unwanted signal reflections. It has a wide bandwidth and thus can carry transmissions that simultaneously pass a great deal of information.

codec. Coder-decoder. A pair of devices for compressing data by encoding it and for decoding the compressed data to obtain the original information. Normally used for reducing the bandwidth required to transmit information.

cofactor. The *cofactor* of an element of a matrix is the matrix that is formed when the row and column containing the element are removed.

For example, the cofactor of the element a_{11} in the matrix

$$\begin{bmatrix} 4 & -5 & 6 \\ 12 & 23 & -8 \\ 2 & 9 & 16 \end{bmatrix}$$

is

$$\begin{bmatrix} 23 & -8 \\ 9 & 16 \end{bmatrix}$$

coherence. 1. The quality of portions of an image having a common relationship. 2. The tendency of adjacent pixels, adjacent scan lines, or successive frames of an animation sequence to have similar color or relative motion. This tendency can be used to develop algorithms that reduce the number of computations required to produce images and thereby speed up the image generating process.

colinear. The fact that two or more points lie on the same line.

collage theorem.   A theorem that is central to generating fractal pictures using *iterated function systems (IFS)*. The theorem says that it is possible to find a set of transformations (contraction mappings) whose IFS will approach a particular image to any desired degree of accuracy.

collimate.   To generate an image that is optically focused so that it appears to be at infinity. This is the image that is easiest for the eye to observe, since the eye muscles are fully relaxed when focusing at infinity.

color. The frequency of emitted light. The human eye records a wide variety of beauty in color, but actually all that is being perceived is differences in the frequency of the observed light.

color burst. A short set of cycles of the chrominance subcarrier in a color television signal. It is used to synchronize the color oscillator frequency in the display system.

color correction. The modification of colors in an image to a more desirable set of values. For example, if a photograph is taken on film balanced for daylight colors using artificial illumination, the colors will be different from the actual colors and will be unpleasing. *Color correction* can be applied to this image to bring the colors back to the original ones observed in the scene.

color cycling. Changing of colors in a video display is such a way as to simulate motion.

color descriptor table. A table that describes a limited number of discrete colors in terms of their red, green, and blue components.

color dithering. Simulating of colors not directly available to a display or printer by the use of varying patterns and sizes of dots of the available colors.

color edging. A line of incorrect color which occurs at the boundary of two colors in a video image. Also called *fringing*.

color electronics prepress system. (CEPS). A system for electronic pagination and imaging for color printing that is computer controlled, using the Neugebauer equations to calculate color values.

Color Graphics Adapter. (CGA). A graphics adapter card that interfaces the IBM PC and compatibles to a color monitor using a low resolution color graphics standard.

color keying. Filming of a picture on a solid color background (usually blue) so that it can be superimposed upon another image to produce a composite picture.

color mapping. The assignment of colors to represent some quality of the data being displayed.

color model. A set of qualities for defining a particular color. See *CMYK, HSB, PMS,* and *RGB*.

color quantization. The reduction of a large number of colors to a limited number of discrete colors through some method of determining which sets of the original colors can be assigned to common colors in the reduced color space.

color reference frame. The specification of the chromaticity of three primary colors as a standard for a color television system.

color separation. The process of separating color images into individual primary color components. When applied to a cathode-ray tube display system, the primary color components are the additive colors red, green, and blue. When applied to color printing, the primary color components are the subtractive colors cyan, magenta, and yellow, with black often used also.

color space. Any three-dimensional space used to represent the qualities of colors.

color table. A look-up table used to translate color index codes into red, green, and blue color components.

colorimetry. The study of the human perception of colors, including attempts to relate human color perception to quantitative measurements.

colorizing. 1. Assigning pseudocolors to an image. 2. Converting a black and white motion picture to color through artistic and/or computerized techniques.

COM. Computer output microfilm. A computer peripheral device which produces computer output directly on microfilm.

comic-mode. Method of recording data on a film strip so that it can be read when the strip is held horizontally.

Commission International de l'Éclairage. (CIE). An international commission on illumination. It is responsible for developing specifications for color matching systems.

compact disk. (CD). A 4-3/4-inch disk upon which digital data is recorded for playback by a laser reader. CDs provide a high-quality method of storing music, since the digital recording technique is immune to noise generated with most other recording techniques. CDs have the capability for storing large amounts of computer data, but currently methods of home recording such disks are not available. Reading of data is also slower than for hard magnetic disks.

compact disk read-only memory. (CD-ROM). A storage system for digital computer data using CDs as the storage medium. As of 1993 a CD-ROM disk holds about 600 megabytes.

compaction algorithm. An algorithm that permits compression of data so that it can be stored in less space.

complete candidate list. A list of graphics objects that is guaranteed to contain the nearest object intersected by a given ray (if one exists).

composite solid. A complex solid object composed from primitive solids using constructive solid geometry.

composite transformation. The translation, rotation, and/or scaling of a vector through the application of a *composite matrix*.

composite video. A video signal in which all color information and horizontal and vertical synchronization signals are combined into a single video output.

composition of matrices. The combining of matrices, each representing a rotation, translation, or scaling, into a single matrix. Applying this *composite matrix* has the same effect upon the original vector as applying each of the original matrices in turn.

compound document. A file that contains more than one type of data (such as text, graphics, voice, and video).

compression. Any software or hardware technique that reduces the storage space required for a set of data.

compression ratio. The size of a block of original data divided by the size of the data after compression.

computer-aided (or -assisted) design (or drafting). (CAD). Software used to assist a designer or draftsman in creating a design and the drawing for it. Normally the output of a CAD program actually produces a drawing on a printer or plotter.

computer-aided (or -assisted) manufacturing. (CAM). A system which can take the output of a CAD program and use it to directly operate machinery to fabricate the part described in the CAD output.

computer-aided software engineering. (CASE). A computer program that permits the computer to generate the details of program code when basic relations are entered into the program.

computer-based training. (CBT). An interactive program which enables the computer to teach a subject. Also referred to as *courseware*.

computer generated imagery. (CGI). Images generated by a computer for display on a computer monitor.

Computer Graphics. Magazine published by the Special Interest Group for Graphics of the Association for Computer Machinery.

Computer Graphics Interface. (CGI). An ANSI/ISO standard currently under development that will be used to establish formats for direct communication of graphics primitives from computers to display devices, printers, and plotters. Also known as *virtual device metafile*.

Computer Graphics Metafile. (CGM). A computer graphics standard that permits interchange of vector and bit-mapped graphics between widely differing computers.

computer imaging. The creation of a picture through the use of computer techniques to generate each pixel of a display image.

computer readable. Data in a format and/or on a medium that can be read directly into a computer.

concave polygon. A polygon in which the sum of the interior angles is greater that 360 degrees. For a *concave polygon* a line can be drawn that will intersect more than two edges.

conceptual model. A description of the properties, features, characteristics, etc., of the thing being modeled.

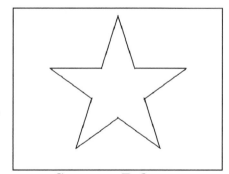

Concave Polygon

cone. A quadric surface that is created by sweeping a line segment around an axis when one end of the line segment is on the axis.

cone tracing. A ray-tracing technique that uses conical regions rather than individual rays of light in order to reduce the total number of computations required to generate an image.

cone plus cosine. An antialiasing filter which uses the sum of a cone and a cosine as the weighting function.

cones. Those receptors in the human eye that respond to bright light and are particularly sensitive to color.

constant angular velocity. (CAV). A method of data recording in which the same amount of data is recorded for each revolution of a disk, even though it would be possible to record more data at the outer edge of the disk than at the inner edge of the disk.

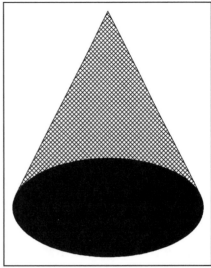

Cone

constant linear velocity. (CLV). A method of disk drive design in which the disk speed is varied with head position so that the linear amount of disk surface passing under the head in a given time is the same for large outer tracks as it is for smaller inner tracks. This permits more data to be stored on the outer tracks.

constructive solid geometry. (CSG). A solid modeling technique that uses Boolean combination of primitive solid objects to construct more complex solid objects.

contention. The attempt by two or more computer devices to access another device. If there is a possibility that *contention* may take place, some *collision avoidance* technique must be used to assure that only one of the contending devices obtains access at a given time.

contextual search. The process of searching files for a particular word or phrase rather than looking for a particular file name.

contiguous. Items that are adjoining.

continuity. The property of a curve such that the magnitude and direction of the derivatives of curve segments at the join point are equal. If this is true for the first n derivatives, the curve is called C^n *continuous*.

continuous image. An image that is defined over a continuous domain, as compared to a *discrete image*, which is defined only for the discrete points within an array of pixels.

continuous potential method. A method for generating the fractal curves of Mandelbrot or Julia sets.

continuous tone. An image, such as a photograph, that may contain all values of gray or color.

contour. A curve which is the locus of points having a value equal to a given constant. The most common example is the contour lines on a map, each of which represents an equal elevation of terrain.

contractive transformation. An affine transformation which decreases the distances between all pairs of points.

contrast. The ratio of the maximum to the minimum intensity of an image.

contrast enhancement transform. A transform that alters the slope of a transform to change the contrast of an image.

contrast threshold function. (CTF). The minimum perceptible contrast for a specific display observer, as a function of spatial frequency.

contribution factor. The percentage contribution of a given ray to the eye ray.

control hull. A graphics construct created by connecting the control points for a bicubic patch that encloses the patch.

control points. The set of points used to define the geometry of a spline, Bezier curve, or patch.

control strips. A series of color bars and percent tints that are placed just outside the actual image area to be used in adjusting ink color to achieve consistent color in color printing.

convergence. Color cathode-ray tubes have a phosphor that consists of many clumps of three dots: one red, one green, and one blue. When the three electron guns that illuminate the three different color dots are properly aligned, the dots will *converge* at the face of the tube, resulting in a dot that is apparently white. The process of adjusting each gun focus to achieve this effect is called *convergence*.

convex. In geometry, the property that any two points within a geometric figure may be connected by a straight line that lies entirely within the figure.

convex decompositions. A technique for dividing an arbitrary polygon into more elementary convex figures, such as trapezoids or triangles.

convex hull. The smallest convex shape that contains a given set of points or objects.

convex polygon. A polygon whose interior angles sum to 360 degrees.

convolution. Application of a convolution integral to a set of data so as to replace each input data item with an output data item that is a weighted sum of neighboring input data values. This usually helps to reduce the noise content of a noisy signal.

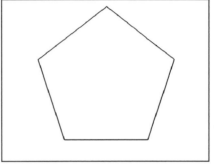

Convex Polygon

convolution kernel. A matrix of weighting values for neighboring pixels to be used in computing a new value for a central pixel.

Cooley-Tuckey algorithm. The original fast Fourier transform algorithm, used for computing the frequency components of a digitally sampled signal with the minimum amount of computation.

Coons patch. A surface that is fitted to four arbitrary boundary curves.

coordinate rotation digital computer. (CORDIC). An iterative fixed-point technique used to compute coordinate rotation, discrete Fourier transforms, exponential, logarithmic, forward and inverse circular, and hyperbolic functions.

coordinate system. A set of references used to locate a position in space. For example, in two-dimensional space, the cartesian coordinate system locates positions with respect to two orthogonal axes, the horizontal x axis and the vertical y axis. In the polar coordinate system, a position is located by specifying its angle θ with respect to the x axis and its distance r from the origin.

coplanar. Two or more points or lines that lie within the same plane.

copy. A duplicate of a disk or tape. If the data are digital, copies of copies may be made with no degradation from the original. If the data are analog, each copy of a copy will be degraded from the one the copy is made from, due to accumulation of noise.

CORDIC. Coordinate rotation digital computer. An iterative fixed-point technique used to compute coordinate rotation, discrete Fourier transforms, exponential, logarithmic, forward and inverse circular, and hyperbolic functions.

corotron. An electrostatic charging device used in electrostatic copying machines or printers.

cosine fractal. A fractal curve produced by iterating the equation

$$z_n = \cos(z_{n-1}) + c$$

with $z_0 = 0 + i0$ and c varied over the complex plane.

cpi. Characters per inch. The density of characters per inch on paper or tape. For characters printed on tape, this is the same as *character pitch*.

cracking. The creation of unintended gaps between polygons that are intended to share edges, caused by lack of sufficient mathematical accuracy.

Cramer's rule. A method for finding an adjoint matrix.

crawling. A result of aliasing in which an edge appears to move discretely from one scan line to the next, rather than moving smoothly.

CRC. Cyclical redundancy checking. An error checking technique in which a checksum is computed for a data block by dividing by some convenient number (usually a power of 2) and taking the remainder. The CRC is saved. When doing error checking, the block CRC is computed again. It must be the same as the saved value if no errors have occurred.

critical angle. The maximum angle at which light passing from one medium is refracted to another. For angles equal to or larger than the *critical angle*, the light is totally internally reflected.

critical fusion frequency. The display refresh rate at which flicker is no longer visible to the human eye. The value is affected by display angular size, display brightness, ambient lighting, and the particular human observer.

cropping. Selecting a portion of an image for use and discarding the rest.

cross-hairs. A type of graphics cursor consisting of horizontal and vertical lines whose intersection is the selected point.

cross-hatch. To fill a region with a pattern composed of uniformly spaced horizontal lines intersected by uniformly spaced vertical lines.

CRT. Cathode-ray tube. A display device used in computers and television sets. The cathode-ray tube consists of an electron gun that projects a beam onto a phosphorescent screen. These are enclosed in a glass envelope, the interior of which is evacuated. The electron beam is focused at the desired spot on the screen by electromagnetic coils mounted external to the tube. The electron beam then excites the phosphor at that point, causing it to emit light.

CSG. Constructive solid geometry. A solid modeling technique that uses a Boolean combination of primitive solid objects to construct more complex solid objects.

CSMA (/CD, /CA). Carrier sense multiple access. A technique for preventing two stations on a network from attempting to access the same device at the same time. With *CMSA* when a station is transmitting, it sends a carrier along with the data transmission. When any other station on the net desires to transmit, it first listens for the carrier and only transmits if there is no carrier present from other stations. This does not completely prevent collisions, however. With *CSMA/CD* (carrier sense multiple access with collision detection) a station continues to listen for a carrier during transmission. If a carrier is detected, both stations stop transmission and retry after a random time. With *CSMA/CA* (carrier sense multiple access with collision avoidance) the same technique is used as with *CSMA/CD* and in addition, data are transmitted with time division multiplexing so that data packets from different stations are unlikely to interfere with each other.

CTF. Contrast threshold function. The minimum perceptible contrast for a specific display observer, as a function of spatial frequency.

cuberille. Of or related to a model used for visualization of three-dimensional data. It divides space into equal-sized parallelopiped volumes and uses data values to construct polygonal faces on selected volumes to render the image.

cuboctahedron. An Archimedean solid having fourteen faces that consist of squares or triangles. Also known as a *nolid*.

CUI. Character-based user interface. A computer system in which user-typed characters are used to control computer operations.

culling. Eliminating data from graphics processing by using relatively simple tests to isolate objects that will be invisible in the finished image.

culling, backface. The process of testing faces of a convex polygonal object and eliminating those that are not visible (as identified by the fact that the normal to the face is pointed away from the screen) so that they do not have to be processed for display.

cursor. A symbol displayed on the computer screen which indicates where an input will have effect.

curve segment. A portion of a curve that lies between two specified points.

CUT. The file extension used to designate a bit-mapped image file in the format specified for the *Dr. Halo* paint program.

cyan. A bluish green color which is one of the primary colors used in subtractive color imaging processes.

cyan, magenta, yellow, and black. (CMYK). The four subtractive colors used in color printing. All colors in a picture are comprised of these four basic colors. Color printing is accomplished by four passes through the printing press, each pass using ink of one of these basic colors.

cyclic overlap. An arrangement of a set of graphics objects such that they cannot be placed in a priority order so that higher priority objects always cover lower priority objects.

cyclical redundancy checking. (CRC). An error checking technique in which a checksum is computed for a data block by dividing by some convenient number (usually a power of 2) and taking the remainder. The CRC is saved. When doing error checking, the block CRC is computed again. It must be the same as the saved value if no errors have occurred.

cycolor. A photographic printing process that makes use of a special film having embedded microcapsules containing colored dyes to permit full color and full tonal reproduction of continuous tone colored images.

cylinder. A quadric surface that is created by sweeping a line segment around an axis when the line segment is parallel to the axis.

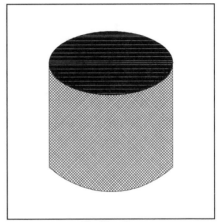

Cylinder

cylinder primitive. A graphics primitive that is used to represent the bonds between atoms in molecular modeling.

cylindrical equal area. A method of projecting a sphere onto a plane in which a unit cylinder is wrapped around a unit sphere and parallels of latitude are projected directly outward along planes normal to the polar axis.

cylindrical equirectangular map. A method of projecting a sphere onto a plane in which the sphere is projected onto an encasing vertical cylinder.

D

D/A converter. Digital-to-analog converter. Converts a set of digital pulses representing a number into an analog voltage whose amplitude is proportional to the digital number. The device must be tailored for a digital pulse train of a particular length, pulse characteristic, and pulse repetition rate.

D1. A format used to encode a video signal as a sequence of binary numbers using eight bits per pixel.

D2. A format used to encode a video signal as a sequence of binary numbers using ten bits per pixel.

da Vinci's postulate. All branches of a tree, at any particular height, have a cross-sectional area, when summed, that is equal to the cross-sectional area of the trunk just below them.

DAD. Digital audio disk. See *compact disk*.

daisy wheel. A rotating wheel with spokes that is used in some printing devices. Each spoke has a character type mounted at its end. The wheel is rotated until the desired character is lined up with the paper and then a hammer forces the spoke against the ribbon, transferring the character image to the paper.

DAL. 1. Data access language. Apple software that converts data bases from other than Apple computers to a form readable by the Macintosh. 2. DAT auto loader. A device which contains a magazine of several DAT tapes, any one of which can be read when desired.

damping. A counter force that causes motion to be slowly reduced to zero.

dark line image. A conventional printed image having dark type on a light background. Same as a *positive image*.

DASD. Direct access storage device. An on-line, directly addressable storage device, such as a floppy or hard disk drive or a CD-ROM or tape player.

DAT. Digital audio tape. A high-quality audio tape recorder/player that records audio signals in digital form, thereby avoiding noise in recording or playback.

data. A group of facts or pieces of information, stored in some format that can be accessed and understood by a computer.

data base. A collection of data arranged in an orderly fashion to permit quick access to any desired datum.

data communications. The movement of data from one isolated system to another. In contrast, *data transfer* refers to movement of data within a single system.

data compression. Any technique for reducing the amount of space required for a particular data set by various means of encoding. Usually used before a data set is stored in order to reduce storage requirements. A compressed data set must be decompressed before use.

data header. A heading for a data set that contains an identifying title and often various format information in some standardized format.

data set. A collection of related data, usually stored in a single file.

data structure. The way in which a set of data is arranged in a file.

data transfer. Movement of data within a single computer.

DCT. Discrete cosine transform. A mathematical technique for image compression in which blocks of pixels are represented by spatial frequencies. The process removes frequencies that have small coefficients.

DDA. Digital differential analyzer. An algorithm used to rasterize a line or curve by recursively using the line slope formula to compute a point on the line in one direction for a unit step in the orthogonal direction and then rounding off to the nearest pixel.

DDS. Digital data storage. A format for sequentially storing data on tape. Usually used for backing up a complete hard disk, since access to a particular file can only be obtained by scanning all the way from the beginning of the tape.

de Casteljau evaluation algorithm. An algorithm for generating a *Bezier curve*.

deallocate. To release a reserved block of memory for use by other applications.

deblock. To extract a single data record from a large block of recorded data.

debounce. Circuitry to read only one input when a switch closure occurs and ignore secondary opens and closures that occur as the switch contacts settle down to their new position.

decal. An image that is mapped to a surface to specify its texture. Also known as a *texture map*.

decimation. The process of changing a sampling rate to represent a signal with fewer samples than were originally used.

decoder. Device or software that converts data in a coded (and usually compressed) form back to the original data state.

decompress. To reverse the procedure used to compress a block of data so as to restore it to its original form for use by a computer.

deep. Having high color saturation and low color value, thereby producing a pure dark color.

defect management. Any technique used to compensate for defects in a recording medium. With hard disks, the first defect management technique is usually to scan the unrecorded disk, locate defective tracks, and lock them out, prohibiting their use for recording. In addition, once the disk is recorded, various checksum methods can be used to restore a few missing or defective bits.

deformation.   An operation that transforms simple shapes to more complex shapes by deforming the space in which the simple shape is embedded.

degausser.   A device for removing unwanted magnetism that accumulates in monitors or tape or disk recording heads.

delimiter.   A character assigned to separate fields in data base records.

DeMoivre's theorem.   A trigonometric relationship expressed by

$$(\cos \theta + i \sin \theta)^n = \cos n\, \theta + i \sin n\, \theta$$

dendrite.   A branching tree-like figure.

densitometer.   A device that measures the transmission characteristics of images, thereby making it possible to obtain a large number of uniformly colored prints.

density.   A measurement of the transmission characteristics of an image on film. *Transmission (T)* is the amount of incident light passed through the image. It is 1 for a completely transparent image and 0 for one that passes no light whatsoever. *Opacity (O)* is the reciprocal of *transmission*. It is 1 for a completely transparent image and infinity for one that passes no light. *Density (D)* is the logarithm (to the base 10) of *opacity*.

depth buffer.   A plane that contains image information, whether or not it is physically located in the same frame buffer that holds the color information for the image. Also known as an *alpha buffer*.

depth cuing.   Reducing an object's color and intensity as a function of its distance from the observer.

depth of field.   The minimum and maximum distances from a camera lens at which the focused image is acceptably sharp.

descenders.   In typography, the portion of a lowercase character that falls below the main part of a letter. The lowercase letters that have descenders are g, j, p, q, and y.

descending sort.   Sorting data backwards, beginning with *z* and ending with *a*.

descriptor. A key word used to characterize the contents of a document so as to permit its retrieval by an automatic sort.

desktop publishing. The creation of quality printed documents using a personal computer. The material to be published is created and stored on the computer and either printed directly on a desktop laser (or similar quality) printer or stored on disk for reproduction by a commercial printing process.

developing agent. The chemical in a photographic developer solution that converts exposed portions of the silver halide emulsion to black metallic silver.

device coordinates. A graphics coordinate system that is an integral part of a device such as a digitizing tablet.

device dependent. A quality (such as the number of available colors) that is characteristic of a particular device and may change if a different device is used.

device driver. A small computer program that conducts communication between the computer and a peripheral device such as a disk drive, a modem, or a printer.

devil's staircase. A stair-like fractal, having steps of different sizes and heights, derived from the Cantor sets.

diazo process. A photographic process that produces positive copies (dark areas reproduced dark, white areas reproduced white) using exposure under ultraviolet light and development with either liquid or gaseous ammonia.

dichotomous branching. The process whereby a tree divides into branches.

diffeomorphism. A mapping in which both the mapping and its inverse are Cantor sets.

differential pulse code modulation. (DPCM). A set of image data compression techniques that makes use of an algorithm for predicting successive data from past data and encoding the differences between the predicted data and the actual data.

diffraction. A deviation from normal propagation of light that occurs when a light wave intersects an object whose features have a size on the order of the wavelength of visible light.

diffuse reflection. A situation in which a light ray incident on an object's surface is absorbed and reradiated after passing through the object. The reradiated light is distributed uniformly. It has its intensity reduced proportionally to the distance it travels through the object. Its color is a combination of the color of the original light and the absorption spectrum of the object's surface.

diffusion-limited aggregation. A method of drawing fractal planar trees.

digital. The storing of data in the form of coded pulses as opposed to *analog*, which is the storing of data as voltage levels.

digital audio tape. (DAT). A high-quality audio tape recorder/player that records audio signals in digital form, thereby avoiding noise in recording or playback.

digital camera. A camera that records an image by first projecting it onto an array of photocells and then storing the information from each cell in the array in digital form.

digital data storage. (DDS). A format for sequentially storing data on tape. Usually used for backing up a complete hard disk, since access to a particular file can only be obtained by scanning all the way from the beginning of the tape.

digital differential analyzer. (DDA). An algorithm used to rasterize a line or curve by recursively using the line slope formula to compute a point on the line in one direction for a unit step in the orthogonal direction and then rounding off to the nearest pixel.

digital dissolve effect. A method of dissolving one image into another when both images are available only in digital form. One such method is to randomly write the pixels of the second image over the first.

digital filtering. Improving the appearance of an image by replacing a pixel by some function of that pixel and its neighbors. Also known as *discrete convolution*.

digital signal processing. A branch of engineering that deals with the relationship between analog signals and their digitally sampled counterparts, together with methods for analyzing and processing the digital signals.

digital video. A video signal encoded as a sequence of binary numbers. See *D1* or *D2*, which are two standard formats for digital video.

digital video interactive. (DVI). A technology for the compression and reconstruction of video images that are stored digitally.

digitize. The process of converting a signal or image into a collection of digital data. The information to be converted is usually scanned in some orderly fashion and the data stored sequentially.

digraph. In typography, two vowels that are joined together to form a single character. Also known as a *diphthong*.

dingbat. In typography, a nonalphanumeric symbol that has the same size as a letter or number such as a smiling face. Type fonts consisting entirely of *dingbats* are available. Using such a font, each letter or number of a standard keyboard will cause an associated *dingbat* to be printed. Also known as a *pi character*.

diophantine. A number α is *diophantine* if there exist $c > 0$ and $v > 0$ such that $|\alpha - p/q| > c/q^v$.

diphthong. In typography, two vowels that are joined together to form a single character. Also known as a *digraph*.

direct access. The capability to access a desired data set directly rather than by means of some indexing scheme.

direct access storage device. (DASD). An on-line, directly addressable storage device, such as a floppy or hard disk drive or a CD-ROM or tape player.

direct image film. A film that produces an image of the same polarity as the image being copied, i.e., a negative image produces a negative copy or a positive image produces a positive copy.

direct port. A hardware device that bypasses graphics accelerators to permit direct reading and writing into the graphics frame buffer.

direct user. A graphics system user who accesses graphics devices directly through the lowest level graphics language in order to obtain maximum speed and efficiency.

direction cube. A method of subdividing space that is used in ray-tracing algorithms. A cube is centered at the origin of the rectangular coordinate system, with the coordinate axes passing through the center of the faces of the cube. The faces are then subdivided into small rectangles.

directional light. A light source that radiates nonuniformly in space, as, for example, a spotlight.

discrete. An electronic component that is a single circuit element such as a resistor, capacitor, inductor, or transistor, as opposed to an integrated circuit that contains a number of these devices on a single chip.

discrete convoluting. Improving the appearance of an image by replacing a pixel by some function of that pixel and its neighbors. Also known as *digital filtering*.

discrete cosine transform. (DCT). A mathematical technique for image compression in which blocks of pixels are represented by spatial frequencies. The process removes frequencies that have small coefficients.

disk. A round flat recording device coated with a suitable magnetic or optical recording medium for the storage of data. Controversy has always existed as to the spelling of *disc* or *disk*. Some sources maintain that the spelling *disc* should only be used for optical media (including compact audio discs) and that *disk* should only be used to refer to magnetic media.

disk array. A combination of multiple disk drives together with software that produces redundant storage so that in the event of failure of a single disk drive, no data are lost. See *RAID*.

disk drive. A device containing motors, electronics, and magnetic heads for reading and writing data to a magnetic disk. A floppy disk drive accepts removable disks. A hard disk drive has one or more magnetic disks permanently built into the unit.

disk management. The control of information stored on a disk through the use of directories and subdirectories.

diskette. A floppy disk.

diskless workstation. A computer with processing capability but no disk storage device of its own. It must be connected to a local area network that permits it to share the disk storage facility of a server station.

display buffer. Memory for storing the data that comprise an image to be displayed.

display device. The component of a display system that converts signals into a visual image, such as a cathode-ray tube or an array of liquid crystal display devices.

display element. A primitive graphics shape that is to be displayed, such as a line, a circle, a sphere, etc.

display file. Data that can be used to display an image, stored as a single file.

display list. A list of display data and commands sufficient to build and display a particular image.

displayable. Capable of being shown on a particular display (having the proper colors, size, etc.).

dissolve. To change from one image to another by superimposing a minimum intensity version of the second image on top of the first and then increasing the intensity of the second image and decreasing the intensity of the first image over time until only the second image is displayed.

distributed ray tracing. A multidimensional form of stochastic ray tracing.

dither matrix. An array of numbers that represents a dithering pattern. This pattern is usually repeated in blocks over the entire screen.

dithering. Simulating gray tones by the use of varying patterns and sizes of black background dots.

D-max. The highest density (darkest image) obtainable for a particular photographic medium.

D-min. The lowest density (lightest image) obtainable for a particular photographic medium.

dodecahedron.   A solid having twelve plane faces. The *regular dodecahedron* has faces that consist of pentagons. The *rhombic dodecahedron* has sides that consist of rhombuses.

domain of attraction. The area of a strange attractor which includes all points which, upon iteration of the attractor's iterated equation, approach a particular point. Same as *basin of attraction*.

dominant wavelength. The wavelength of monochromatic light that can be mixed with white light to match a given color. The *dominant wavelength* doesn't have to be a component of the given color.

doming. Outward change in the shape of the shadow mask of a cathode-ray tube caused by heating by the electron beam. The result is errors in color purity as different colored dots that are supposed to superimpose on the screen surface no longer do so. This limits the maximum luminance that can be produced on a region of the display unless sophisticated corrective measures are employed.

dot. 1. A display of one pixel. 2. A circular marker of selectable size on an image.

dot cloud.   A set of dots used in molecular modeling to represent transparent surfaces.

dot leaders. A series of dots that fill the space between two items on the same line, as between a table of contents descriptive item and the corresponding page number.

dot matrix. A printer whose printing mechanism is a column of solenoid-actuated pins that produce dots on the paper. By actuating the proper combination of solenoids for each column, characters or graphics may be produced.

dot pitch. The distance between two phosphor dots of the same color on adjacent lines on a cathode-ray tube screen.

dots per inch. (dpi). A measure of the quality and resolution of a display or printer. This is the number of horizontal or vertical dots that can be displayed or printed in a linear inch.

Douady rabbit. The Julia set for $c = -0.12256 + i0.74486$.

double buffer. In graphics, an arrangement of memory such that one portion of memory can be used to store an image that is currently being displayed while a new image is being constructed in another portion of memory. When the new image is complete, switching occurs so that the new image is displayed and another image is constructed in the part of memory that was initially being used for display.

double scan. A technique used to allow the VGA to produce low- resolution images in a format designed for the CGA. Each horizontal line of data for a 200-line image is drawn twice to give a 400-line image.

DPCM. Differential pulse code modulation. A set of image data compression techniques that make use of an algorithm for predicting successive data from past data and encoding the differences between the predicted data and the actual data.

dpi. Dots per inch. A measure of the quality and resolution of a display or printer. This is the number of horizontal or vertical dots that can be displayed or printed in a linear inch.

dragging. Moving a graphics object through the use of software that enables the user to position a cursor on the desired object through use of a mouse or trackball and then depress a button to cause the graphics object to follow a path directed by the mouse to a new location.

dragon curve. A fractal curve that is a plot of the set representing the result of iterating the equation

$$z_{n+1} = cz_n(1 - z_n)$$

DRAM. Dynamic random access memory. Integrated circuit memory that uses the charge in a capacitor as the memory storage medium. This simplifies the memory elements so that high storage density at low cost can be achieved. However, since the charge on the capacitor slowly leaks off, it must be refreshed periodically in order to preserve the stored information.

drop out. A defective section of magnetic media on which data cannot be recorded.

dry processing. A technique for developing a latent photographic image without chemical treatment.

dry silver film. A nongelatin silver film emulsion which is processed by heat rather than chemicals.

Duff's formulation. A method of curve interpolation using control points.

dump. A printout of raw data contained in a file.

DVI. Digital video interactive. A technology for the compression and reconstruction of video images that are stored digitally.

Dvorak keyboard. A keyboard layout invented by August Dvorak that is supposed to arrange the letters and characters for fastest and easiest typing. The standard QWERTY keyboard was deliberately designed to slow up typing speed so as not to exceed the capabilities of original typewriter mechanisms.

dyadic. Of the form $p2^{-k}$.

dye polymer recording. An optical storage technology which uses a laser beam to record data on layers of dyed plastic.

dynamic beam focusing. A means of modifying the focusing current applied to the electron beam of a cathode-ray tube so as to compensate for beam length differences as the beam traverses the screen, so as to have the beam always in focus at the screen surface regardless of distance changes.

dynamic random access memory. (DRAM). Integrated circuit memory that uses the charge in a capacitor as the memory storage medium. This simplifies the memory elements so that high storage density at low cost can be achieved. However, since the charge on the capacitor slowly leaks off, it must be refreshed periodically in order to preserve the stored information.

dynamic range. 1. The ratio of the maximum level of a signal to the minimum level. 2. The dynamic range that an electronic circuit is capable of handling.

E

EBCDIC. Extended binary coded decimal interchange code. An 8-bit code used for alphanumerics and characters. Developed by IBM for use in large mainframe computers.

ECC. Error correction code. A coding technique that permits recovery of a block (2048 bytes) of data that is read incorrectly from a CD-ROM.

EDCA. Error detection and correction. A technique for assuring that data are correctly written to a storage device. It requires writing a prearranged extra block of data after each block of regular data. The prearranged block is then read. If it is correct, the regular data block is also assumed to be correct. If not, an error is assumed and the regular data block and prearranged block are rewritten.

edge. The curve that marks the intersection of two surface primitives or that marks where a surface primitive ends.

edge detector. A first derivative filter used to sharpen digitized images.

edge merging. The process of filling in the gaps caused by *cracking*, resulting in an image without objectionable gaps.

EDIF. Electronic data interchange format. A standard format for exchanging CADDS data defined in *Electronic Design Interchange Format, Version 2:0.0, EIA Interim Standard No. 44*, May 1987, ISBN 0-7908-000-4.

editable PostScript. PostScript language commands translated into a text file that can be edited without reference to the software which originally generated the PostScript file.

EEPROM. Electrically erasable programmable read-only memory. A memory chip that is designed so that it can be programmed with data which remain until erased, regardless of whether the chip is powered.

EGA. Enhanced Graphics Adapter. A display interface for the IBM and compatible PCs. The EGA is capable of displaying 16 colors at a resolution of 640 × 350 pixels.

electrically erasable programmable read-only memory. (EEPROM). A memory chip that is designed so that it can be programmed with data which remain until erased, regardless of whether the chip is powered.

electromagnetic deflection. A method of positioning the beam of a cathode-ray tube by using the magnetic field produced by orthogonal coils of wire (the deflection yoke) positioned around the neck of the cathode-ray tube.

electron gun. The device in a cathode-ray tube which generates a stream of electrons that impinges upon and thereby activates the phosphors that make up the screen, thus causing them to emit light.

electronic forms. Graphics that are merged with data to form a single display.

electronic publishing. The process of producing and providing documents in an electronic form.

electronically programmable logic device. (EPROM). A memory chip in which the memory cells, when programmed electronically, hold the data continuously, regardless of whether the device is powered, until the data are erased by exposure to intense ultraviolet light through a window on top of the chip package.

electrophotographic printing. A printing technology in which light projected on an electrically charged drum removes the charge from selected areas of the drum. Toner is applied to the drum, where it sticks only to the noncharged portions. Paper is then pressed against the drum, causing the toner to transfer to the paper. The paper is then heated to permanently set the toner. Used in copying machines and laser printers.

electrostatic deflection. A method of positioning the beam of a cathode-ray tube by applying an electric field to deflection plates that are built into the cathode-ray tube. Only a few special cathode-ray tubes have such deflection plates built in.

electrostatic discharge. (ESD). Static sparks produced by discharging a high voltage built up by friction. Accidental ESD from humans to integrated circuit chips can cause substantial damage to the chips.

electrostatic printing. A printing technology that uses a special paper which is electrically charged in selected areas by an electron beam. Toner is applied to the paper, sticking only to the charged areas. The toner is then fixed by application of heat. Used in large-image copiers and plotters.

ellipse.   An oval two-dimensional figure defined by the equation

$$\frac{x^2}{R_x^2} + \frac{y^2}{R_y^2} = 1$$

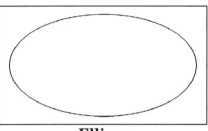
Ellipse

ellipses. Three equally spaced dots used to indicate omitted material in quoted text.

ellipsoid.   An egg-shaped solid defined by the equation

$$\frac{x^2}{a^2} + \frac{y^2}{b^2} + \frac{z^2}{c^2} = 1$$

elliptical torus. The solid generated by sweeping an ellipse about a given axis.

em. In typography, a square space that is a space having the same width as the height of the type font. In traditional type faces, this is the width of a capital *M*, but this is not necessarily true for all modern type faces.

embedding plane. The plane containing a polygon that one wishes to test for intersection by a ray.

emboss. To raise in relief from a surface.

embossing. A printing techinque in which text is raised above the surface of the paper.

emittance. Pertaining to light emitted by a surface.

emulsion. A light-sensitive photographic coating over film or paper. Most emulsions consist of light-sensitive silver salts suspended in gelatin.

en. In typography, a space that is half the width of an *em*. In traditional type faces, this is the width of a capital *N*, but this is not necessarily true for all modern type faces.

encapsulated PostScript image. A *PostScript* language file that contains, in self-standing form, all of the information needed to produce an image. Such images are compatible with almost any hardware or software capable of understanding the *PostScript* language.

encapsulation. Enclosed, as within a capsule.

enclosure. A surface that surrounds another surface.

encoder. 1. An electronic device that takes separate red, green, and blue signals produced by a color television camera and combines them into a composite video signal for television transmission. 2. A software package that converts statements in a computer language into assembly language commands that can be processed by hardware. 3. A device for compressing data.

end of file. (EOF). A special character that indicates the end of a file.

Enhanced Graphics Adapter. (EGA). (Trademark of IBM Corp.). A display interface for the IBM and compatible PCs. The EGA is capable of displaying 16 colors at a resolution of 640×350 pixels.

environment. The volume of space enclosing a scene that is to be ray traced and the collection of graphics objects contained therein.

environment map. An image, often computed as a projection on a cube, used to reduce computation in rendering of reflecting surfaces. It is produced by first computing each point of an image as a function of the direction from the center point of the object and then referencing the image to the directions of reflected rays from the surface of the object.

environmental bound. A simple convex volume that surrounds the ray-tracing environment. When a ray passes through the *environmental bound* it can never again enter the environment, so that further intersection testing is unnecessary.

EPROM. Electronically programmable logic device. A memory chip in which the memory cells, when programmed electronically, hold the data continuously, regardless of whether the device is powered, until the data are erased by exposure to intense ultraviolet light through a window on top of the chip package.

EPS. Encapsulated PostScript. A file that includes the complete description of graphics and text in the PostScript language. Such a file contains all of the information that is needed for a PostScript printer to print the graphics and text data.

equalizing pulses. Pulses that are a part of the vertical retrace portion of a television signal. They are used with the signal for an interlaced display to enable odd frames to start at the beginning of a horizontal scan line and even frames to start at the midpoint of a horizontal scan line.

equicontinuous. A family $F = \{f_\alpha\}$ of continuous functions is *equicontinuous* if, for any $\xi > 0$, there is $\delta = \delta(\xi, z)$, such that $|f_\alpha - f(_\alpha(\omega)$, when $|z - \omega| < \delta$.

equipollent forces. Forces that result in the same net force and torque.

equipotential. A closed curve representing points of equal potential.

error correction code. (ECC). A coding technique that permits recovering a block (2048 bytes) of data read incorrectly from a CD-ROM.

error detection and correction. (EDCA). A technique for assuring that data are correctly written to a storage device. It requires writing a prearranged extra block of data after each block of regular data. The prearranged block is then read. If it is correct, the regular data block is also assumed to be correct. If not, an error is assumed and the regular data block and prearranged block are rewritten.

error diffusion dithering. A dithering technique in which the error in approximating a given pixel is used to bias the values of nearby pixels so as to balance out the error. Also known as *error propagation dithering*.

ESD. Electrostatic discharge. Static sparks produced by discharging a high voltage built up by friction. Accidental ESD from humans to integrated circuit chips can cause substantial damage to the chips.

Ethernet. A digital data network for connecting personal computers using a single coaxial cable. Originated by Xerox Corporation.

exhaustive testing or **exhaustive ray tracing.** The testing of a ray for intersection with every graphics object in a scene.

explicit surface. A surface where each point on the surface is defined by evaluation of a set of parametric equations.

extended binary coded decimal interchange code. (EBCDIC). An 8-bit code used for alphanumerics and characters. Developed by IBM for use in large mainframe computers.

Extended Graphics Adapter. (XGA). An IBM standard graphics adapter that supports resolutions up to 1024 pixels by 768 pixels.

extended light source. A source of illumination in the description of a scene to be rendered as a graphics image, in which the light is emitted from a finite surface rather than a point.

extent. The minimum and maximum values of a graphics object in each of the coordinate directions.

extent test. A test of whether a ray intersects an extent. If it does, further testing is necessary to determine whether the ray intersects the graphics objects within the extent; if it does not, there is no intersection and no further testing is necessary.

extinction coefficient. A measure of absorption of light passing through a translucent medium.

eye point or **eyepoint.** The viewpoint.

eye ray. A ray that begins at the eye point and passes through the display screen.

eye-readable. Images recorded on a microfilm which can be read without magnification. These are usually in the form of headings which enable the user to determine whether he or she has the right microfilm reel before inserting it into the microfilm reader.

F

face. A polygon that is part of a three-dimensional graphics object.

face boundary. The edge of a face polygon that is shared with an edge of another face polygon.

face curve. The intersection of an implicit surface with a proximate interval's face.

face normal. A vector that is perpendicular to the surface of a face. It usually is normalized (the vector is set to have a length of 1).

facet. One of a number of flat surfaces that together make up a solid object.

faceting. The irregular appearance of a three-dimensional object when it actually has a smooth surface, but for simplicity is represented by a number of facets.

facsimile. A technology that converts a paper document to a digitized image, transmits the digital data to a remote device (usually via phone lines), and converts it to a paper document which duplicates the original at the remote.

factorial polynomials. Polynomials defined in a form that permits discrete analogs of Taylor's formula.

fading. A technique for simulating the appearance of atmospheric haze in images. Each pixel of the image is mixed with a color that is exponentially weighted according to the distance of the object from the observer. The color is usually white for daylight scenes and black for night scenes.

falloff. The decrease in intensity of light from a spotlight as a function of the angle from the beam center.

false coloring.   1. The assignment of frequencies outside the visual spectrum to frequencies within the visual spectrum. 2. Assignment of colors other than the natural object colors to objects in an image. Usually accomplished through the use of a color table. 3. Producing unavailable colors by dithering of colors that are available.

false contours.   Changes in color intensity or hue that are caused by quantization errors, but appear to the observer to be contour lines.

Farey tree.   A tree structure of numbers that includes each rational number between 0 and 1 exactly once.

fast anamorphic image scaling.   A technique for remapping an image by stretching, rotation, skewing, or rescaling.

fast Fourier transform.   An algorithm for computing the frequency components of a digitally sampled signal with the minimum amount of computation. The original algorithm for this purpose is known as the *Cooley-Tuckey algorithm*.

fast Phong.   A simplified technique for Phong shading that reduces the amount of computation required by evaluating the Phong shading at vertices and then interpolating to obtain a value for a particular point on a face.

FAT.   File allocation table. An area on a disk which shows the tracks and clusters assigned to each recorded file.

fat fractal.   A fractal derived from the Cantor sets that has nonzero measure for certain projection directions.

fatbits.   An option in the Macintosh graphics program *MacPaint* that allows the user to enlarge and alter a bit-mapped image.

Fatou set.   The complementary set to the Julia set using complex numbers.

fax.   Short for *facsimile*. A technology that converts a paper document to a digitized image, transmits the digital data to a remote device (usually via phone lines), and converts it to a paper document which duplicates the original at the remote.

fax-back. A technology that permits a user to call a phone number, respond to voice prompts to conduct a document search, and have the selected document sent to a fax machine.

FCC. Federal Communications Commission. The United States government agency responsible for establishing wireless transmission specifications, assigning frequencies for transmission, and establishing limits on spurious transmissions by electronic equipments.

FDDI. Fiber distributed data interface. An interface to a wide bandwidth fiberoptic digital data network.

FDM. Frequency division multiplexing. A technology that divides the available frequency bandwidth of a transmission line into narrower frequency bands, each of which can be used to transmit an independent voice conversation or data stream. This increases the number of transmissions that can be sent simultaneously over a single transmission line.

feature extraction. An optical character recognition technique in which unique features of each character are stored in a table so that the optical scanner can compare a scanned character with the stored features and thereby identify it.

Federal Communications Commission. (FCC). The United States government agency responsible for establishing wireless transmission specifications, assigning frequencies for transmission, and establishing limits on spurious transmissions by electronic equipments.

Feigenbaum constant. A number equal to 3.678573510..., which often marks the boundaries of chaotic behavior.

Fermat primes. Prime numbers found by the formula

$$p = 2^{2^n} + 1$$

ferric chrome. A layer of mixed ferric oxide and chromium dioxide particles that makes up the recording medium for a tape or disk.

ferric oxide. A layer of ferric oxide particles that makes up the recording medium for a tape or disk.

Feshner's law. The basic scientific law regarding perceived response. It states that the perceived response to a sensory stimulus is proportional to the logarithm of the intensity of the stimulus.

fiber distributed data interface. (FDDI). An interface to a wide bandwidth fiberoptic digital data network.

fiberoptic cable. A cable consisting of thin strands of glass through which data are transmitted in the form of light. The bandwidth of a fiber optic cable is orders of magnitude larger than for wires or coaxial cables, thereby allowing simultaneous transmission of many more simultaneous sets of data than for a wire or coaxial cable or bundle of the same size.

Fibonacci number system. A set of numbers developed from the recursion relationship

$$F_{n+2} = F_{n+1} + F_n$$

fiche. Short for microfiche.

field. 1. In a data base, an individual item of information, such as name, address, etc. A set of fields make up a data record. 2. The data that make up one vertical scan of a cathode-ray tube.

field frequency. The number of video fields that are displayed in one second.

field-of-view. The solid angle in space which may be viewed from an observer position (and is therefore shown on a display of the scene).

field rendering. The rendering on a display of the scan lines that make up only one field of an interlaced display.

field separator. A code or character used to separate the fields of a record. Also known as a *delimiter*. The most common field separator is the comma.

FIFO. First in, first out. A method of handling data in which the first item to be stored is also the first item to be read out.

file. A set of related data, stored in a computer or a storage medium such as a disk or tape, and referenced by a single file name.

file allocation table. (FAT). An area on a disk which shows the tracks and clusters assigned to each recorded file.

file extension. In MS/DOS, file names may consist of up to eight characters followed by a period followed by up to three more characters. The characters following the period are known as the *file extension*.

file format. The manner in which data are arranged within a file.

file protection. Any technique for preventing the accidental erasure of a data file. Removable disks are file protected by covering a notch on the disk with tape or sliding a switch.

fill. To apply color to the interior of a closed figure in a graphics image.

filled-in Julia set. The set, J_c, of initial values z_0 for which the values of z_n in the Mandelbrot equation are bounded for a given parameter c. The Julia set proper consists of the boundary points of J_c.

film plane. Synonym for *focal plane*.

filter. 1. To electronically change a signal by changing the relative amplitudes of its component frequencies. 2. To select certain specified types of data from a file.

finite element modeling. To divide a mechanical object into small, cubic sections, so that each section can be analyzed separately.

firmware. Computer code that is stored permanently in a ROM or integrated circuit chip.

first in, first out. (FIFO). A method of handling data in which the first item to be stored is also the first item to be read out.

fish-eye lens. An extremely wide angle lens, characterized by considerable image distortion.

fixed disk. A hard disk. The disk and drive are an integral unit that is permanently installed in the computer. The disk cannot be removed from the drive.

fixed spacing. In typography, a type font in which all of the characters have the same width. In contrast, proportional spacing describes a type font where narrow letters such as *i* or *l* use much less space than wide letters such as *m* or *w*.

fixing. 1. In photography, the chemical process by which unexposed silver salts are removed from a film or print so that the developed image will remain unchanged for a long period of time. 2. In electrostatic printing, the application of heat to fuse the toner permanently to the paper.

flat shading. A technique for producing the illumination effects on graphics objects in an image. Each graphics primitive is divided into a number of polygon surfaces and a single appropriate color is used to fill each polygon.

flatbed plotter. A plotter which makes use of a carriage containing a number of pens that moves over a sheet of paper mounted on a flat surface.

flatten. To convert a hierarchical data structure into a single nonhierarchical list.

flattened display list. A display list that has only a single level of hierarchy.

flicker. A perceived rapid variation in the intensity of a displayed image, caused by the refresh rate being too slow for a given observer and set of lighting conditions.

flight simulation graphics. A set of software that displays a simulation of the images seen when flying an aircraft and allows the user to interface with the displays by operating various controls as if he or she were flying the aircraft.

flood filling. A technique for filling a connected two-dimensional region with a color or pattern, in which a point is selected within the polygon, and the color or pattern is extended in all directions until the polygon boundary is encountered. Algorithms for flood filling need to be carefully designed to make sure that all parts of peculiarly shaped polygons are filled. Also known as *seed filling*.

Floyd-Steinberg filter. An algorithm for performing discrete convolution or digital filtering, which is the improving of the appearance of an image by replacing a pixel by some function of that pixel and its neighbors. The *Floyd-Steinberg filter* is also often used to change color images to images consisting of black, white, and shades of gray.

flying spot scanner. A technology in which a document is scanned by a point of light to convert it into electronic signals.

focal distance. The distance in front of a camera at which objects are in sharpest focus.

focal length. The distance from a lens to the focal plane when the lens is focused at infinity. The focal length of a normal 35-mm camera lens is 50 mm. Lenses having longer focal lengths are known as telephoto lenses and those having shorter focal lengths are known as wide angle lenses.

focal plane. The plane or surface on which a lens focuses to produce a sharp image.

focal point. The point at which light rays converge to a point after passing through the lens. The locus of *focal points* is the *focal plane*.

focus. 1. The position at which light rays from a lens converge to produce a sharp image. 2. The process of changing the distance between the lens and the focal plane so that the image on the focal plane becomes as sharp as possible.

focus servo. A device in an optical drive that keeps the read/write light beam aligned with the tracks regardless of imperfections in the disk surface.

folder. A term used by Macintosh for its file management technique. A folder is analogous to a directory or subdirectory in DOS.

Foley and van Dam. One of the classic reference books on computer graphics, *Computer Graphics: Principles and Practice* by James Foley and Andries van Dam.

font. A set of characters, letters, and digits of the same type style and size. When moveable type was common, a font consisted of a certain number of pieces of type for each character, the number depending upon the frequency with which each character was used. (For example, a font contained a lot more *e*'s than *z*'s.) With electronic type fonts a font refers to only a single occurrence of each character.

footcandle. A unit of illuminance. Originally the light on a surface per unit area produced by a standard candle. The *footcandle* is now defined as 10.76 lux.

footlambert. A unit of luminance (the photometric brightness of a surface). One footlambert is equal to 3426 nits.

formatted data. A data file that is set up with a particular structure and that usually includes titling, indexing, and job separation instructions.

formatting. The preparation of a data storage medium such as a disk or tape by defining tracks, sectors, and filling them with a null character.

forward differencing. An iterative method for obtaining a set of points on a surface by evaluating a bicubic function. The *forward difference* is the amount that the function changes when the argument is incremented by a specified step.

forward ray-tracing. A ray-tracing technique in which every light ray is traced in the same direction that it normally travels. Since most light rays never have any effect on the image produced on the screen, forward ray-tracing techniques are very wasteful of computer time and resources.

4:2:2. A method of encoding pixel color information where 8 bits are allowed for each pixel, with 4 bits used for luminance, 2 bits for the *I* color component, and 2 bits for the *Q* color component.

Fourier transform. A formula used to convert a sampled analog signal into its frequency components.

foveal vision. Vision through the high-resolution center portion of the eye. The total resolution of the human eye is approximately 512×512 pixels, but the resolution is not uniform, with the largest number of pixels concentrated close together at the center of the eye and the remaining pixels distributed more widely around the periphery.

fractal. A curve whose Hausdorff-Besicovitch dimension is larger than its Euclidian dimension and which has elements of self-similarity. Thus, for example, a curve that consists of a large number of line segments should have the Euclidian dimension of 1, which is a line. If this curve winds around in such a way that it fills all of the space available in a plane, then we would intuitively like to associate it with a dimension of 2, which is the dimension of a plane. Such a curve is a fractal and has a Hausdorff-Besicovitch dimension of 2. Mandelbrot claims that in the same way that Euclidian shapes, such as circles and squares, are the natural way of describing man-made objects, fractals are the natural way of describing objects that occur in nature such as mountains and trees.

fractal dimension. The Hausdorff-Besicovitch dimension of a fractal.

frame. The border of the picture area of a display.

frame buffer. A hardware device that provides an interface for a frame of computer data to the monitor. It contains memory to store the color of each pixel together with circuitry to manage input to the memory and output in a form that can be accepted by the monitor.

frame grabber. A device that converts a video picture into a digital file.

free-form. An image that is drawn by hand without use of rulers, triangles, or other mechanical devices.

Frenet frame. A reference frame consisting of a unit length tangent, T, to the central axis; a principal normal, N; and a binormal, B.

frequency. The number of recurrences per unit time of a periodic phenomena.

frequency aliasing. An aliasing effect that results from limited sampling of the visible light frequency spectrum. It manifests itself as incorrect colors for objects that are ray traced.

frequency division multiplexing. (FDM). A technology that divides the available frequency bandwidth of a transmission line into narrower frequency bands, each of which can be used to transmit an independent voice conversation or data stream. This increases the number of transmissions that can be sent simultaneously over a single transmission line.

Fresnel equation. An equation that expresses the attenuation of a reflected beam of unpolarized light from a surface as a function of angle of incidence of the light upon the surface, the wavelength of the light, and the properties of the reflecting surface.

fringing. A line of incorrect color which occurs at the boundary of two colors in a video image. Also called *color edging*.

frisket. In publishing, an area of a piece of artwork that is protected from modification.

frustum of vision. The volume within which graphics objects are viewed and processed to form an image. It is bounded by planes that intersect at the viewpoint.

f-stop. The ratio of the focal length of a lens to its aperture diameter.

full duplex. A data communications method that allows simultaneous transmissions in both directions over a communications link.

fusing. In electrostatic printing, the process of permanently attaching the toner to the paper through the use of heat.

fuzzy rug. A technique for producing an image where the gray-scale intensity of the image is proportional to height. Also known as a *waterfall*.

G

gain. The factor by which a signal is increased by an electronic amplifying device.

gamma correction. A technique for compensating for the nonlinear response of a cathode-ray tube display. The intensity of light emitted by the cathode-ray tube phosphor is proportional to the applied grid voltage raised to the *gamma* power, where *gamma* may range from 2.3 to 2.8, depending upon the cathode-ray tube characteristics. A correction is needed to provide proper contrast to the image. In television signals, this compensation is applied before transmission.

gamut. The complete range of colors that can be produced by a display device . This includes luminance and chromaticity.

gamut mapping. Converting color data designed for a display device having a particular gamut to a new gamut suited for another display device.

Gantt chart. A type of bar chart used to plan a project and track the progress and resources used to accomplish the project.

garbage in, garbage out. (GIGO). An expression indicating that if the input data are worthless, the output data will be worthless also.

garbled. The corruption of data.

Gaussian blur. The deliberate introduction of blur into an image through the use of a Gaussian filter to produce the effect of a photograph of a moving object. Note that in real life, such blur is not a property of the scene being viewed, but is produced by the motion of the image of the moving object across the film plane during the time while the camera shutter is open.

Gaussian filter. A filter used for weighting contributions to a pixel in anti-aliasing. It has the equation $p = 2^{-2x^2}$. The Gaussian 1/2 and Gaussian $1 / \sqrt{2}$ filters use the same equation multiplied by 1/2 and $1 / \sqrt{2}$ respectively.

gaze direction. The direction in which the observer of a ray-traced scene is looking.

GDDM. Graphical data display manager. Graphics software for IBM mainframes that accepts scanned data and provides outputs to terminals, plotters, printers, etc.

GEM. Designation for paint and drawing programs that are produced by Digital Research Corp. They make use of image storage files having the *IMG* extension. Such files store monochrome or 16-color images in a run length encoded format.

generalized cylinder. The surface that is generated when a two-dimensional contour is swept along a three-dimensional trajectory.

generalized ray. A light element used in ray tracing that is more sophisticated than a single primitive ray of light, such as a beam or a cone.

generative helix. The mathematical expression that creates such spiral patterns such as those that occur on pinecones or pineapples.

generator. A curve composed of connected straight line segments that is used to repeatedly replace each straight line segment in a curve to create a self-similar fractal.

genlock. The capability of a video display device to lock its output to a set of incoming synchronization signals. In television, the display is locked to horizontal and vertical synchronization signals that cause the image to remain stable on the screen.

geodesic. A great circle path that gives the shortest distance between two points on the surface of a sphere.

geographic information system. (GIS). A system for storage, retrieval, and manipulation of maps and other geographic data.

geoid. The figure of the earth; the mean sea level conceived as extended continuously through all the continents.

geometric continuity. A joint between two curve sections whose tangent directions are equivalent at the joint. The two sections will appear to form a smooth curve.

geometric normal. The surface normal at a particular point on a surface as computed from the geometric characteristics of the surface at that point, as contrasted to the *shading normal*, which the user can set to a different value to modify shading effects.

geometric object. A two- or three-dimensional shape.

geometric optics. A branch of optics that studies the interaction of light with geometric objects that are much larger than the wavelength of light.

geometric primitive. A basic geometric shape that is mathematically defined for treatment by a rendering program.

geometry. The branch of mathematics that studies the relations, properties, and measurement of solids, surfaces, lines, and angles.

geospecific texture. A texture derived from aerial or satellite photographs that is mapped onto a terrain model.

ghosting. The appearance of a secondary displaced image on a television screen due to reflections of the television signal that arrive at the receiving antenna displaced in time from the primary signal.

GIF. Graphics interchange format. A file format developed by CompuServe for compressing and storing graphics image data. Also the file extension given to files in this format.

giga. 1 billion. In ordinary mathematics the prefix *giga* denotes that the following quantity is multiplied by 1 billion, but in computer terminology, the prefixes *kilo, mega, giga*, etc. represent successive multiplications by 1024 rather that 1000 so that *giga* is actually 1,073,741,824.

gigabyte. 1,073,741,824 bytes of data. See *giga*.

gigaflop. One billion floating point operations per second.

GIGO. Garbage in, garbage out. An expression indicating that if the input data are worthless, the output data will be worthless also.

gingerbreadman. A fractal curve produced by iterating the equations

$$x_{n+1} = 1 - y_n + |x_n|$$
$$y_{n+1} = x_n$$

GIS. Geographic information system. A system for storage, retrieval, and manipulation of maps and other geographic data.

Gingerbreadman

GKS. Graphical kernel system. A graphics software program standard for producing two-dimensional images. Provides outputs for line graphics devices such as plotters or raster graphics devices such as monitors or printers. Specified by ANSI standard X3.124-1985.

global parameterizability. The characteristic of an implicit curve contained in a proximate interval Y of having at most one point in Y on the curve for any value of the ith parameter.

gnomonic projection. A projection of a sphere onto a plane where the projection is accomplished through rays that begin at the center of the sphere. Also known as *central projection*.

golden mean. A proportion that is found to create geometric figures that are pleasing to the eye. It is $\tau = (\sqrt{5} + 1)/2$.

Gosper curve. A self-similar fractal generated by the initiator-generator method which has a fractal dimension of 1.1292.

Gouraud shading. Producing a smooth variation of surface intensity over a triangle or quadrilateral by bilinearly interpolating the intensities from the vertices.

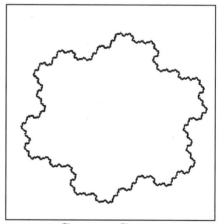

Gosper Curve

gradient. In graphics, the smooth blending from one color to another.

graftal. A class of graphics objects similar to fractals, but generated with a set of rules that permits local modification of properties.

granularity. The resolution of an image as limited by pixels in a display, grains consisting of silver clumps in a potographic film or print, or photoreceptors in the human eye.

graphical data display manager. (GDDM). Graphics software for IBM mainframes that accepts scanned data and provides outputs to terminals, plotters, printers, etc.

graphical kernel system. (GKS). A graphics software program standard for producing two-dimensional images. Provides outputs for line graphics devices such as plotters or raster graphics devices such as monitors or printers. Specified by ANSI standard X3.124-1985.

graphical user interface. (GUI). A computer control system which permits the user to use a pointing device such as a mouse or trackball to position a cursor at one of a number of options shown on a computer screen and then activate a selection device such as a mouse button to cause the computer to perform a desired set of actions.

graphics interchange format. (GIF). A file format developed by CompuServe for compressing and storing graphics image data. Also the file extension given to files in this format.

graphics mode. A display mode in which each pixel can be accessed and colored separately, as contrasted to *text mode*, in which only a set of predetermined characters can be displayed.

graphics object. One or more geometrical primitives grouped for convenience in rendering.

gravity. The use of an implied region around a preexisting graphics object in two-dimensional graphics so that when a vertex for a new object is created within the *gravity* region, it will be placed at the nearest point on the preexisting object.

gray ramp. A display showing an ordered progression of shades of gray from black to white.

gray scale. The number of shades of gray that can be produced by a graphics system.

great circle. A path along the surface of a sphere where all points on the path are intersections of a plane through the center of the sphere and the sphere's surface.

greeking. The representation of a page layout using bars and boxes to represent groupings of text.

grid. An array of horizontal and vertical lines used to locate particular objects in a graphics image.

grid location. A system of letters and numbers assigned to the rows and columns of a grid respectively to permit location of a desired object.

grip. An area near the edges of a printed page that is reserved for mechanical devices that hold the paper in place during printing and therefore cannot be printed upon.

groove. A continuous channel designed into a recording medium to guide the reading device.

Guckenheimer's example. A Julia set constructed using the equation $R(z) = (z\text{-}2)^2/z^2$.

GUI. Graphical user interface. A computer control system which permits the user to use a pointing device such as a mouse or trackball to position a cursor at one of a number of options shown on a computer screen and then activate a selection device such as a mouse button to cause the computer to perform a desired set of actions.

Gupta-Sproull algorithm. A technique for drawing antialiased lines. The algorithm draws three pixel wide lines using the Bresenham algorithm. It determines the proper pixel color by determining the perpendicular distance from the pixel center to the line center and then using a table lookup.

gutter. In publishing, the inside margins between facing pages of a book or magazine, which often include extra space to allow for binding.

H

H & J. Hyphenation and justification. The arrangement of the spacing between words of text so that it begins and ends evenly at the margins. This includes breaking up words at the appropriate syllable breaks (hyphenation) to avoid wide spaces that might occur if a large word doesn't quite fit on a line.

Hadamard matrix. An $n \times n$ matrix of elements equal to +1 or -1 and whose rows and columns are mutually orthogonal. Used in applying the *Hadamard transform*.

Hadamard transform. A formula used to convert a sampled analog signal into its frequency components. Similar to but less well known than the *Fourier transform*.

halation. Reflections from outside a cathode-ray tube or within the glass face plate that limit the maximum contrast that may be obtained between neighboring pixels.

half duplex. A data communications technique in which transmission can take place in either direction along a line, but only in one direction at a time.

half phase filter. A filter that uses an even number of samples, thereby producing an output that is situated between two input samples. Compare with *zero phase filter*.

half-plane. One half of a plane. Normally a plane extends from $-\infty$ to $+\infty$ in the x direction and $-\infty$ to $+\infty$ in the y direction. The *half-plane* extends from 0 to $+\infty$ in the x direction and $-\infty$ to $+\infty$ in the y direction.

halftone. A graphic in which dots are used to represent continuous tones, with large, closely spaced dots representing darker areas and smaller, widely spaced dots representing lighter tones. This permits the printing of photographs on paper using ordinary printing processes, which cannot handle continuous tone images. A *halftone* can be created from a photograph by rephotographing it through a screen that breaks the picture up into dots.

haloed line. A line that is part of a group of intersecting lines and which is drawn continuously while the other intersecting lines are drawn with gaps at the intersection points.

Hamilton system. An energy-conserving physical assembly.

handle. A small rectangle on a computer image that indicates the spot where a mouse cursor can be placed to manipulate the image.

handling zone. The part of an optical disk that can be touched by the disk drive's gripping mechanism.

handshaking. The exchange of information at the beginning of a data communications session during which two communicating systems determine the specifications such as parity, baud rate, speed, etc., which are to be used for the session.

handwriting recognition. Computer software for converting hand-written material into machine-readable text.

hard copy. Data, text, or graphics printed on paper rather than residing on a disk or in a memory, from which it must be viewed by display on a monitor. Compare with *soft copy*.

hard disk. A magnetic storage device making use of a disk coated with magnetic material that is an integral part of the disk drive mechanism. Contrast to *floppy disk* where the disk is removable from the drive. *Hard disks* can have more precise tracking control and thereby store more data in a given area than floppy disks.

hard error. An error in data communications or on a disk that cannot be corrected with the data correction methods used by the system.

hard hyphen. A hyphen that will always appear in the reproduced text. A *soft hyphen* will only be printed or displayed if it comes at the end of a line.

hard return. In word processing, a carriage return that is entered by the user and that causes the succeeding text to move to the beginning of the next line, regardless of whether the current line is full.

hard sectored. A floppy disk that has the sector boundaries permanently marked, such as by punching holes in the disk at the sector boundaries.

hard space. A specially designated space character used instead of an ordinary space between two words to make it impossible for a line break to occur between the two words. If the two words occur at the end of a line, they will either both be on the current line or both moved to the next line.

hardware. Electronic circuitry designed to perform computer operations.

hardwired. Computer option that is permanently set into a computer at the time of installation and cannot easily be changed by switches or software.

Harter-Heightway dragon curve. A fractal curve drawn using the L-systems or initiator-generator technique which has the appearance of a dragon.

hash total. Sum of the data in an information field (often modula some number) used to provide a checksum that can be used to determine data accuracy at a later time.

hashing function. A function that associates a key value with an entry (or index) in a table.

Harter-Heightway Dragon

Hausdorff dimension or **Hausdorff-Besicovitch dimension.** A dimension greater than the Euclidian dimension which appears to more correctly express the dimensional characteristics of fractal curves. For self-similar fractals where line segments are replaced repeatedly by a generator having N line segments each of which is of length r, where r is a fraction of the line segment being replaced, the *Hausdorff dimension* is

$$D = \frac{\log N}{\log \frac{1}{r}}$$

Hausdorff distance. The distance between two closed bounded subsets of a set.

haze. Smoke, dust, or water droplets which obscure visibility by reducing the contrast of objects when the *haze* is interposed between the viewer and the objects.

HDTV. High-definition television. A television system having much higher resolution than the current standards. The exact specifications for such a system have not yet been standardized.

head. An electronic device designed to read data from a magnetic disk. The head consists of a coil wrapped around a core of magnetic material that contains a small gap. When the gap passes over the magnetized regions of a disk, pulses of magnetic energy occur which are translated into electrical impulses in the coil.

head thrashing. Rapid back and forth movements of a disk head caused by inability of the head positioning mechanism to locate the proper position for the head.

head tracking. A specialized display system in which the position of the observer's head is measured and used to control the viewpoint of a scene displayed on a screen.

headline. In typography, a line of display type at the top of a job. Used to attract attention.

Heckbert's algorithm. An algorithm for color quantization using a median-cut technique.

hedgehog. A three-dimensional object displayed as a wire frame with associated normal vectors.

Heisenberg's uncertainty principle. The principle that the more accurately one measures one quality of an object the less accurately is it possible to measure its other qualities simultaneously.

hemi-cube. The mapping of a hemisphere onto the surface of a cube.

hemi-cube algorithm. An algorithm for calculating radiosity solutions for complex environments.

Henon attractor. The attractor produced by the recursive formulas

$$x_{n+1} = y_n - a * x_n^2 + 1$$

$$y_{n+1} = b * x_n$$

Hermite polynomial. A polynomial used in three-dimensional interpolation.

Hermite polynomial fractal. A fractal curve created by iterating a Hermite polynomial equation over the complex plane.

Hermite splines. A method of generating a bicubic surface using four control points. The first and third control points are used for interpolation. The second and fourth control points are vectors that determine the tangency of the curve at interpolated points.

Hershey fonts. A set of standard character forms developed by the U.S. Bureau of Standards. Now in the public domain.

Hertz. (Hz). A measure of frequency equal to one cycle per second.

heterogeneous model. A model whose elements may have behaviors that differ qualitatively from each other over time.

heterogeneous network. A network that connects computers which have different architectures.

hex. Short for hexadecimal. A numerical system in which 16 digits are used instead of 10. The digits 0–9 are used as for a normal system and the letters A through F are used to represent counts of 10 through 15 in the decimal system. The result is that higher order numbers in the hexadecimal system have a different meaning than in the decimal system. For example, 10 in the hexadecimal system is the same as 16 in the decimal system. In either system we use the convention that we begin counting by using all of the available symbols. When we run out, the next count is represented by the first symbol with a 0 at its right. Thus in the decimal system we can count to 9 with the available symbols. The next count is 10. In the hexadecimal system we can count to F (15 in decimal) and the next count is 10.

hexcone color solid. A color space used to define colors. It consists of a solid that has a hexagon having red, yellow, green, cyan, blue, and magenta on its vertices, white at the center of the hexagon and black directly below the center.

HFS. Hierarchical file system. The file management system used in DOS which allows a disk to have directories that are divided into subdirectories that are divided into subsubdirectories, etc.

hidden line. In graphics, a line on a three-dimensional object that cannot be seen when the object is represented two dimensionally.

hidden line removal. A software process that produces a wireframe rendering of a three-dimensional object in which lines representing surfaces that would be invisible to the viewer are removed.

hidden page animation. An animation technique that requires several pages of display memory, only one of which is displayed at any given time. The background image is stored on a secondary hidden page. To create a new frame, it is transferred to the primary hidden page and the graphics array drawn on top of it. This page is then displayed; the original display page becomes the primary hidden page, and the process is repeated for the next frame.

hidden surface algorithm. An algorithm that determines which surfaces of a three-dimensional object are invisible to the viewer and does not paint these on the screen.

hidden surface problem. The problem of determining which surfaces of a three-dimensional object are invisible to a viewer and therefore should not be shown in a two-dimensional mapping of the object.

hidden surface removal. The process of applying a *hidden surface algorithm* to identify and remove invisible surfaces.

hierarchical configuration. A collection of objects organized into a tree hierarchy with the position and orientation of each object's frame described in the coordinates of its parent.

hierarchical file system. (HFS). The file management system used in DOS which allows a disk to have directories that are divided up into subdirectories that are divided into subsubdirectories, etc.

hierarchical structure. A series of objects or items divided or classified in ranks or orders.

hierarchy. A system of organizing a number of elements into a tree. Each element of the hierarchy is known as a node. When two nodes are in the hierarchy, the higher one is called the parent and the lower one the child. A node with no parent is a root. A node with no children is a leaf.

hierarchy traversal. The traversal of a hierarchy of bounded volumes forming a tree for efficient determination of collision of a ray with an object in ray tracing.

high coherence. The characteristic of an image where adjacent pixels are very likely to be of the same or nearly the same color.

high-definition television. (HDTV). A television system having much higher resolution than the current standards. The exact specifications for such a system have not yet been standardized.

high density. Floppy disks that have a greater capacity that the normal capacity of disks of that dimension. For example, normal density 5¼-inch floppy disks have a capacity of 360K bytes; high-density 5¼-inch floppy disks have a capacity of 1.2 megabytes. Similarly, normal density 3½-inch floppy disks have a capacity of 720K bytes and high-density 3½-inch floppy disks have a capacity of 1.44 megabytes.

high resolution. A display or printer image that has the number of pixels or dots per inch increased from the number normally used so as to produce a better quality image.

highlight. A bright region on the surface of an image of a shiny object resulting from a specular reflection from a light source.

highlighting. Making the surface of a graphics object brighter to make it stand out from other objects.

Hilbert curve. A space-filling fractal curve of the Peano family of curves.

histogram. A bar chart that shows the distribution of colors or gray shades in an image.

hither. A clipping plane which is perpendicular to the line of sight. It is used to remove objects that won't appear in the image because they are behind the viewpoint or too close to it.

Hilbert Curve

HLS color model. Hue, lightness, saturation. A three-dimensional model for defining color characteristics. It is based on artists' pigments, with *hue* representing the color of the pigment, *lightness* representing the amount of white included, and *saturation* representing the amount of pigment. This model is easy to use, because it is similar to the way humans intuitively classify color. Also known as the *HSL color model*.

Hobby's polygonal pens. A method of drawing wide lines using polygons defined by integer offset vectors.

hollow fill. A rendering of graphics objects in which only the pixels adjacent to polygon edges are displayed.

hologram. A recording on film of the image of an object illuminated by a laser beam. Because of the monochromatic nature of the laser light, the hologram can include much more image data than an ordinary picture, including three-dimensional data.

homogeneous coordinates. A generalization of three-dimensional Euclidian space in which an additional vector is added to the coordinate description. This results in 4×4 transformation matrices which can represent rotation and translation in a single matrix.

homogeneous network. A network that connects computers that all have the same architecture.

homogeneous transformation. An affine transformation defined by a 4×4 matrix.

homograph. A word having the identical spelling of a word in another language.

Hopf bifurcation. The behavior of a recursive equation in which a fixed point becomes unstable and gives birth to an invariant circle, which is attractive.

horizontal retrace. The portion of a video signal during which the scanning electron beam is moved from the end of one scan line to the beginning of the next. Video is usually blanked during *horizontal retrace* so that retrace lines do not appear on the screen.

host. A processor in a multiprocessor system that manages requests for services, resources, or memory from other processors.

HPGL. Hewlett-Packard graphics language. A language used to describe a drawing in a form that can be understood and translated directly into drawing actions by a plotter.

HSB color model. Hue, saturation, brightness. A three-dimensional model for defining color characteristics. It is based on artists' pigments, with *hue* representing the color of the pigment, *saturation* representing the amount of pigment, and *value or brightness* representing the amount of white included. This model is easy to use, because it is similar to the way humans intuitively classify color. Also known as the *HSV color model*.

HSL color model. Hue, saturation, lightness. A three-dimensional model for defining color characteristics. It is based on artists' pigments, with *hue* representing the color of the pigment, *saturation* representing the amount of pigment, and *lightness* representing the amount of white included. This model is easy to use, because it is similar to the way humans intuitively classify color. Also known as the *HLS color model*.

HSV color model. Hue, saturation, value. A three-dimensional model for defining color characteristics. It is based on artists' pigments, with *hue* representing the color of the pigment, *saturation* representing the amount of pigment, and *value or brightness* representing the amount of white included. This model is easy to use, because it is similar to the way humans intuitively classify color. Also known as the *HSB color model*.

Hubbard tree. An algorithm for developing a Julia set by calculating the external angles.

hue. The frequency or wavelength of a color.

hue, saturation, brightness. (HSB). A three-dimensional model for defining color characteristics. It is based on artists' pigments, with *hue* representing the color of the pigment, *saturation* representing the amount of pigment, and *brightness* representing the amount of white included.

Huffman encoding. A method of compressing data through replacing frequently recurring data strings with shorter codes.

hull. A graphics construct that encloses another (usually more complex) graphics construct. For example, straight lines, connecting the four control points for a Bezier curve form a *hull* that encloses the Bezier curve.

Hurst exponent. A measure of the persistence of statistical phenomena.

hyperbola. A curve that is the locus of a point which moves so that the difference of its undirected distances from two fixed points is constant. It has the equation

$$\frac{x^2}{a^2} - \frac{y^2}{b^2} = 1$$

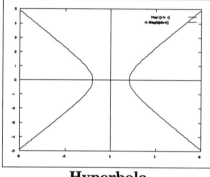

Hyperbola

hyperbolic cosine fractal. A fractal curve produced by iterating the equation

$$z_n = \cosh(z_{n-1}) + c$$

with $z_0 = 0 + i0$ and c varied over the complex plane.

hyperbolic paraboloid. A three-dimensional object whose surface is the locus of all points on the equation

$$\frac{x^2}{a^2} - \frac{y^2}{b^2} = z$$

hyperbolic sine fractal. A fractal curve produced by iterating the equation

$$z_n = \sinh(z_{n-1}) + c$$

with $z_0 = 0 + i0$ and c varied over the complex plane.

hyperboloid. The three-dimensional object produced by rotating a hyperbola around an axis. The *hyperboloid of one sheet* has the equation

$$\frac{x^2}{a^2} + \frac{y^2}{b^2} - \frac{z^2}{c^2} = 1$$

The *hyperboloid of two sheets* has the equation

$$\frac{x^2}{a^2} - \frac{y^2}{b^2} - \frac{z^2}{c^2} = 1$$

hypercube. The analog of a cube in a space of greater than three dimensions. In n-space, a hypercube has $2n$ faces and 2^n vertices.

hyperface. The face of an n-dimensional solid where n is greater than three.

hyperfocal distance. The distance to the nearest object that is in focus when a lens is focused at infinity. If the lens is focused at the hyperfocal distance, everything from half the hyperfocal distance to infinity is in focus.

hyperlattice. An n-dimensional lattice, where n is greater than three.

hypermedia. A technique for delivering information that provides a large number of interconnections throughout the body of the data so that the user can easily jump from a topic to a related or supplementary topic.

hyper-rectangle. A rectilinear region in parameter space.

hypervoxel. The equivalent of a voxel in n-dimensional space, where n is greater than three.

Hz. Abbreviation for hertz. A measure of frequency. One hertz is one cycle per second.

I

I. The in-phase component of a color that is encoded in the *YIQ* color space. The *I* component is the orange-cyan component. See *YIQ space*.

icon. A small picture on a computer screen which designates the area in which a mouse cursor is to be placed to activate a particular program.

icosahedron. A 20-sided solid whose faces are triangles.

ID. Identifier. A name for an object.

ideal inclusion function. A function that provides the tightest bound possible for an object but still permits easier determination of when collisions between light rays and the object occur.

identifier. (ID). A name for an object.

identity matrix. A matrix having 1's on the diagonal and 0's elsewhere. When it multiplies (or is multiplied by) a second matrix, the second matrix is unchanged.

IFS. Iterated function system. The repeated application of a contractive affine transformation, starting with any point, until a distinctive pattern is produced. A few carefully selected contractive affine transformations are sufficient to reproduce a picture having a great deal of detail. Thus the process can be used for image compression.

IGES. Initial graphics exchange specification. A standard file format for the storage and interchange of graphics data. Published by the U.S. National Institute of Standards and Technology.

illuminance. The flux density in lumens per square meter or lux, striking an illuminated surface.

illuminant. A light source whose color spectrum is specified. Needed to assure that comparison of colors is not biased by different light source colors.

illumination. The complete description of all light striking a designated point on a selected surface.

illumination model. The algorithm or equation used to determine the shading of a particular point or surface. Also known as a *shading model* or *lighting model*.

illumination ray. A ray that carries light from a light source to an object.

image. A representation of a picture or graphic, particularly on a computer screen.

image analysis. The identifying and grouping into objects of features in an image and classifying of the objects in order to provide a basis for understanding image content.

image plane. The plane or surface on which a focused lens forms a sharp image.

image processing. The class of processing operations that modify a pixel image.

image resolution. The quality of an image as given by the number of pixels in the horizontal and vertical directions that fill a screen or as the number of dots per inch printed by a printer.

imaging system. A collection of units used to capture and recreate an image. As a minimum, such a system should include a scanner or camera, a device for digitizing the analog image and storing it in memory, a computer for processing digital image data, and a display device such as a monitor or printer.

IMG. The file extension used to designate a graphics file format for bit-mapped images used by *GEM Paint* and *Halo DPE*.

immediate mode. A graphics rendering technique in which each object is rendered immediately upon input rather than being added to a list of objects that are all rendered later.

impact printers. Printers in which letters are formed by selections from a set of vertical pins impacting an ink-impregnated ribbon to transfer the ink to the paper surface. Such printers are inexpensive, but noisy and limited in resolution.

implicit surface. A surface that consists of the locus of all points satisfying a given equation or set of equations.

inbetweening. 1. (v.) The computation of graphics objects that form intermediate steps between an initial image and a final image. Used especially in animation when the beginning and end frames of a sequence are known but additional frames must be inserted between these to produce the apparent action. 2. (n.) A frame produced by inbetweening.

inches per second. (ips). Measure of speed of a magnetic tape system.

inclusion function. A function that bounds an object to permit easier determination of when collisions between light rays and the object occur.

inclusion isotony. The property that if A and C are subsets of B and D, respectively, then $A{\times}C$ is a subset of $B{\times}D$.

incremental backup. The process of backing up only files that have been changed since the last backup, rather than all available files.

incremental spacing. The ability of a printer to adjust character spacing by very small amounts. Most commonly used to adjust the size of spaces between words so as to permit justification of a page of text.

index of refraction. The ratio of the angle of incidence of light upon a surface to the angle of refraction for light entering a medium from a vacuum. It is also equivalent to the ratio of the speed of light in the medium to the speed of light in a vacuum.

indexed color. A number representing an entry in a look-up table that gives a full description of the color. *Indexed colors* may be changed simply by modifying the look-up table.

indifferent periodic orbit. A periodic orbit for which the absolute value of the eigenvalue is one.

information float. The amount of time between the acquisition of data and its availability for use by a user.

initial graphics exchange specification. (IGES). A standard file format for the storage and interchange of graphics data. Published by the U.S. National Institute of Standards and Technology.

initialize. To prepare a device for use, such as by loading an operating system into a computer.

initiator. In the initiator-generator method of creating fractal curves, the *initiator* is the initial geometric structure around which the fractal is built. It may consist of a single line or several line segments that may be formed into a simple polygon such as a triangle, a square, or a hexagon.

ink jet. A printer that produces characters by spraying a fine jet of ink through selected holes onto a sheet of paper.

input devices. Physical or electronic devices which are capable of reading input information and transferring it to a computer. Examples are mice, trackballs, scanners, and modems.

input-indexed color. A technique for identifying colors in which the indexed colors are looked up in the table and converted to detailed color information before being stored in a buffer.

inside-outside function. A function whose result differentiates among points that are inside an object, points that are on the surface of the object, and points that are outside the object.

instance. An object that belongs to some class.

instantiation. Definition of a graphics object in such a way that it may be used repeatedly at different locations in an image without fully redescribing it each time it is used.

intensity. Brightness.

intensity cueing. The variation of light intensity throughout a scene to simulate depth. The intensity of light from a light source varies as the square of the distance from the source. Thus all objects, near and far, in a sunlit scene have nearly the same intensity because the square of the 93 million or so miles of the sun from each object in the scene is almost the same. In contrast, for a scene lit by a local light source such as a lamp, far objects should be darker than close objects. This is in accordance with what we see daily and thus gives us the illusion of depth, which would be absent if the scene were produced with constant light intensity. However, the falloff in intensity produced by the square of the distance produces a scene in which the distant objects are too dark, so computer-generated scenes usually make the falloff proportional to distance or to the square root of distance from the light source.

interactive video. A video program stored on CD-ROM or laser disk that permits a user to manipulate the course of action. Often used as a teaching aid, the program will ask a question of a student and then select the next material to be displayed depending upon whether the student gave the right answer.

interface. The surface defined by the meeting of two different media.

interlace artifact. Flicker resulting when adjacent scan lines of an interlaced display are of different colors.

interlaced. A display system in which one frame consists of only odd display lines and the next of only even display lines, etc. The persistence of the eye makes it appear as if the full picture is being displayed continuously. This reduces the amount of information required for a given resolution by one-half.

interleaved. A system of writing to a hard disk that assigns contiguous sector numbers to noncontiguous sectors on the disk so that after a sector is written or read, enough space is left on the disk before the next contiguously numbered sector for the computer to complete processing of the data and be ready to process the next sector.

intermittency. The situation in a fractal curve where the orbits of singular values go far away and then return.

internal cost. The average cost of solving for the point of intersection of a ray with an object, given that the ray is known to have hit the object's bounding volume.

International Standards Organization. (ISO). A group that establishes standards for graphics, image processing, and telecommunications.

Internet. An extensive computer network that links computers of colleges, universities, government agencies, nonprofit laboratories, and industry. Developed and managed by the Defense Advanced Research Project Agency.

internode. In a tree, a segment that is followed by at least one more segment.

interpenetration. An arrangement of two or more graphics objects such that the surfaces of the objects mutually intersect in a way that cannot be specified explicitly.

interPhong shading. A shading technique that is a modified version of Phong shading which gives a shading intermediate between faceted shading and Phong shading.

interpolate. To determine the value of an intermediate term by averaging or otherwise operating upon neighboring terms that are known.

interrupt. A signal sent by a peripheral or some other part of a computer to the processor that causes the processor to suspend its current operation and run a designated service routine.

intersection. 1. In constructive solid geometry, the three-dimensional region common to two or more specified objects. 2. In ray tracing, a point that is on a surface and also on a particular ray.

invariant circle. A circle where, if one selects an initial point on the circle and performs iterations of a recursive equation, all iterated points will also be on it.

inverse color map. A map used to translate full RGB colors into a limited set of colors.

inverse iteration method. A method of creating the graphic for a Julia set by computing the backward orbits of points.

inverse mapping. The process of determining the parameters for the explicit representation of a surface that contains a designated point.

inverse-square law. A law of physics which states that the intensity of illumination is inversely proportional to the square of the distance between the light source and the illuminated surface.

inversion. A mapping technique that uses a reference circle to map all the points of a plane (except the center point of the reference circle) onto a plane by drawing a line from the center of the circle to the point to be mapped and then placing the new point on this line so that the product of the distance from the center of the circle to the original point and the distance from the center of the circle to the new point is equal to the square of the radius of the circle.

invert. 1. To reverse a binary number so that all ones become zeroes and all zeroes become ones. 2. To reverse a photographic image so that blacks become white and whites become blacks. Intermediate shades are also reversed. This occurs when an image is produced by projecting light through a negative onto a sheet of light-sensitive paper.

ion deposition. A printing method similar to laser printing. A drum is charged with electrons, the charged portions of the drum attract toner, and paper is then pressed against the drum, picking up the ink.

ips. Inches per second. Measure of speed of a magnetic tape system.

IRE units. Units of video signal amplitude, where 100 is maximum white, 7.5 is black, and 0 is blanking black.

irradiance. The light coming onto a surface from other surfaces in the scene, measured by integrating over a hemisphere above the surface.

ISO. International Standards Organization. A group that establishes standards for graphics, image processing, and telecommunications.

isometric projection. A perspective projection in which all vertical lines remain vertical. Distances in the x and y directions are usually drawn at a 60-degree angle to the vertical.

isotropic. A random field in which all points and all directions are statistically equivalent.

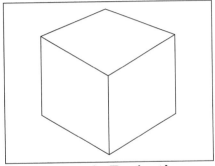

Isometric Projection

italic. In typography, a typeface in which the letters are slanted or cursive.

iterated function system. (IFS). The repeated application of a contractive affine transformation, starting with any point, until a distinctive pattern is produced. A few carefully selected contractive affine transformations are sufficient to reproduce a picture having a great deal of detail. Thus the process can be used for image compression.

iteration. 1. (n.) A single solution of an equation that is to be solved many times. 2. (v.) To repeatedly operate upon an equation that uses the current values of one or more variables to determine new values. At each repetition, the new values obtained in the previous *iteration* are substituted for the old values.

J

Jacobian matrix. A matrix used to generate corrections in a rendered image so that the viewpoint correlates with the point at which a reference photograph was taken.

jaggies. Artifacts of aliasing. The stairstepped appearance of diagonal lines and curves displayed on a device that has only discrete pixel locations.

Jarvis, Judice, and Nanke filter. An algorithm for performing discrete convolution or digital filtering, which is the improving of the appearance of an image by replacing a pixel by some function of that pixel and its neighbors. It is frequently used to change color images to images consisting of black, white, and shades of gray.

jitter. 1. Jumping of a display, usually due to poor synchronization. 2. Random displacements in time of a periodic signal from the temporal position that it should occupy.

jitter function. A function used to deliberately introduce jitter into a sampling process to reduce aliasing effects.

join surface. A surface added to provide continuous transition between two intersecting surfaces in a graphics model. Same as *blend surface*.

joint. The point at which two consecutive segments of a spline curve meet.

Jordan curve theorem. The fact that a simple closed curve partitions the plane into two disjoint regions, a bounded interior and an unbounded exterior, with the curve separating the two. Used to determine whether one is inside or outside a closed curve.

Ray Tracing of an Art Gallery. Image courtesy of Christopher D. Watkins of ALGORITHM, Inc., Atlanta, GA.

Ray Tracing of "Break". Image courtesy of Christopher D. Watkins of ALGORITHM, Inc., Atlanta, GA.

"Steel Mill." A complex environment shaded using progressive refinement radiosity. Courtesy of John Wallace and Stuart Feldman, PCG, Cornell University.

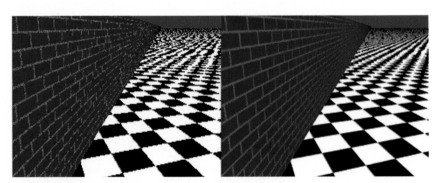

Antialiasing Example. Notice that the image on the left is of very poor quality; this is due to having a discrete number of pixels to represent the image. The image on the right shows the effects of antialiasing. Image courtesy of Christopher D. Watkins of ALGO-RITHM, Inc., Atlanta, GA.

Rendering. This image was created using Pixar's RenderMan® and VG Shaders™, VG Looks™ libraries and the VALIS Prime Rib™ from the Valis Group. Image copyright © 1992 the VALIS Group; RenderMan® image created by the VALIS Group.

Dream Flight. This image was generated with the GenWorld toolkit, using Graflist for the rendering. Copyright © 1988 by Brian Gardner. Reprinted by permission.

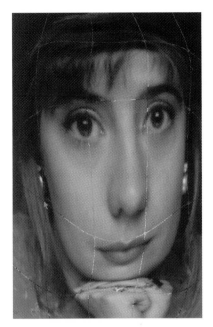

Warping. This is an example of spline warping. Image courtesy of Christopher D. Watkins of ALGORITHM, Inc., Atlanta, GA.

Warping. This is another example of spline warping without the spline mesh. Notice that broadening the man's shoulders caused the bike's spokes to warp as well. Image courtesy of Christopher D. Watkins of ALGORITHM, Inc., Atlanta, GA.

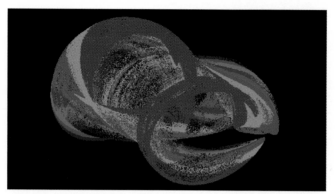

Strange Attractor. Produced by iterating equations $x = \sin(2.24y) - z\cos(.43x)$, $y = z\sin(-.65x) - \cos(-2.43y)$, $z = \sin(x)$. Roger Stevens.

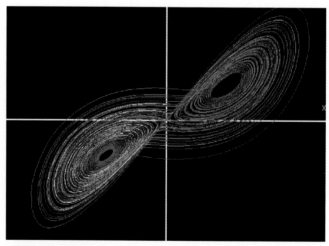

Lorenz Attractor. Produced by iterative equations (*see* attractor, Lorenz). Roger Stevens.

Scene from the Computer Animation "Going Bananas." All of the objects in the room were modeled using an early version of GENMOD. Rendering was accomplished by ray tracing a polygonal approximation to each object. Image courtesy of John Snyder, *Generative Modeling For Computer Graphics and CAD,* Academic Press, 1992.

3-Dimensional Figures. 3-dimensional quadric shapes generated by ray tracing. Roger Stevens.

Ray Traced Images. Ray traced images of cone and reflecting and transparent spheres using POVRAY ray tracing program. Roger Stevens.

joystick. A graphics input device consisting of a vertical rod or handle which can be made to tilt in any direction. When the *joystick* is tilted, the cursor moves in the tilt direction.

JPEG. A proposed standard for image compression developed by the Joint Photographic Experts Group. This standard is also sanctioned by the International Standards Organization (ISO) and the Comité Consultatif Internationale de Télégraphique et Téléphonique (CCITT).

jukebox. A device that holds a number of optical disks and contains one or more optical disk drives. Any disk can be selected for use by a software command.

Julia set. A fractal curve set which is a plot representing the result of iterating the equation

$$z_{n+1} = z_n^2 + c$$

with c held constant and z_0 varied over the complex plane. Compare with *Mandelbrot set*.

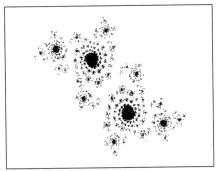

Julia Set

justification. The process of aligning lines of text for printing. *Left justification* makes sure that the left side of every line is lined up. *Right justification* makes sure that the right side of every line is lined up. *Center justification* lines up the exact center of each line.

K

K. Kilo, when used as a prefix. In computing, *kilo* is 1024; in dealing with money, *kilo* is 1000.

Kantor tree. A fractal curve generated by the IFS method.

Kbyte. Kilobyte. 1024 bytes of data.

kd tree. *k*-dimensional tree. A binary subdivision of *k*-dimensional space, one dimension at a time.

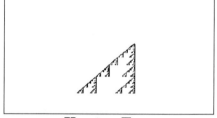

Kantor Tree

kermit. A protocol for transmitting files from one computer to another across telephone lines.

kerning. The use of certain letter pairs that have the space between them minimized to replace the pair of letters in ordinary type.

key. 1. A word or phrase that is used to identify the subject matter of a data file. 2. The buttons on a keyboard that are pushed to transmit alphanumerics or characters. 3. The black primary in color printing.

keyframe. One of a sequence of images in computer animation from which intermediate images are derived by minor modifications to the *keyframe*. See also *inbetweening*.

kinetic depth effect. The rotating of an object about its central axis to give the illusion of three dimensionality because the perspective causes nearer portions of the object to move quicker and in the opposite direction in screen space from more distant portions.

knot. A point in parametric space that is part of the definition of a spline curve.

Koch curve. One of a family of curves similar to the Koch snowflake, but using different generators.

Koch snowflake. A self-similar fractal curve created using the initiator-generator technique. It has an appearance similar to a snowflake.

Kochanek–Bartels formulation. A method for curve interpolation that provides control over tension, bias, continuity, and approximation.

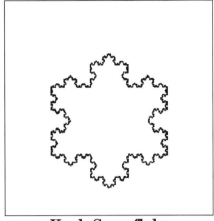

Koch Snowflake

Kolomyjec's organic illusion. An early computer-drawn picture created by Kolomyjec.

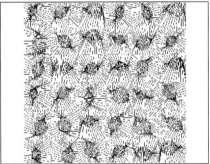

Kolomyjec's Organic Illusion

L

L*. L-star. Lightness.

label. An identifying word assigned to a disk.

lacunarity. A characteristic of fractal texture in which the fractal has gaps that tend to be large or include large intervals such as disks or balls.

ladder. Typeset text having several consecutive lines that end with hyphenated words. This should be avoided for good appearance.

Laguerre fractal curve. A fractal curve generated by iterating a Laguerre function over the complex plane.

lambert. A unit of luminance.

Lambertian radiosity model. A model that uses the radiosity technique to characterize ideal diffuse reflective surfaces.

Lambert's cosine law. The rule that the intensity of light reflected from a point on a surface is proportional to the cosine of the angle between a vector from a point to the light source and the surface normal at the point.

Lambert's law of absorption. The rule for absorption of light in homogeneous media. It states that

$$I_x = I_0 e^{-(Ax)}$$

where I_x is the intensity of the light after passing through the distance x in the medium, I_0 is the intensity of the light as it enters the medium, and A is the absorption coefficient.

LAN. Local area network. Computer boards or external boxes, cables, and software used to connect two or more computers so that they have access to each other's resources.

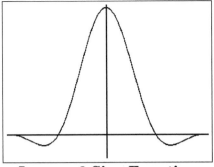

Lanczos2 Sinc Function   **Lanczos3 Sinc Function**

Lanczos2 sinc function. A two-lobed filter function used in antialiasing. It is defined by

$$
Lanczos2(x) = \begin{cases} \dfrac{\sin(\pi x)}{\pi x}\dfrac{\sin(\pi \frac{x}{2})}{\pi \frac{x}{2}}, & |x| < 2 \\[4mm] 0, & |x| \geq 2 \end{cases}
$$

Lanczos3 sinc function. A three-lobed filter function used in antialiasing. It is defined by

$$
Lanczos3(x) = \begin{cases} \dfrac{\sin(\pi x)}{\pi x}\dfrac{\sin(\pi \frac{x}{3})}{\pi \frac{x}{3}}, & |x| < 3 \\[4mm] 0, & |x| \geq 3 \end{cases}
$$

land and groove. A feature manufactured into optical disks during manufacture to identify track locations. The recordable tracks are within the grooves and the lands separate the grooves from each other.

Landsberg fractal curve. A fractal curve constructed by positive midpoint displacements.

landscape. Arrangement of type and graphics on a page so that text is readable when the page is oriented so that its width exceeds its length. Also called *comic*.

laser disk. An optical disk using the same technology as a CD-ROM, but with a diameter of 12 inches.

laser fax. A laser printer that can also be used as a fax machine.

laser optical. A technique for recording on grooveless disks through the use of a laser-optical-tracking pickup to determine head location.

laser printer. A printer that makes use of a beam of light to charge a drum. The charged portions of the drum then pick up toner which is transferred to a sheet of paper and fused permanently by heat.

laser projector. A video projector that makes use of three laser beams, one for each primary color, combined into a single beam that is mechanically scanned to provide a raster on a screen.

last in, first out. (LIFO). A method of storing data in which the last piece of data to be stored is the first one to be read. Also known as a *stack*.

latitude. Distance measured in degrees north or south of the equator. Lines of equal latitude are circles parallel to the equator.

layer. A portion of a graphics image designed so that several *layers* may be overlaid to produce a complete image.

lazy evaluation. A programming technique for minimizing the calculations needed to handle large data structures. The program assumes that such structures exist, but only calculates necessary parts on demand.

LCD. Liquid crystal display. A display that consists of a thin layer of a special liquid sandwiched between two glass plates. Application of a voltage through a pair of transparent conductors causes the molecules of the liquid at the affected location to align with the applied field, changing the optical properties of the liquid. A liquid crystal display does not generate light; it must be viewed by reflected light or by backlighting.

lead screw. A highly accurate screw which is used to position the optical heads of laser disk or CD-ROM drivers to produce spiral recording tracks with uniform spacing.

leader. 1. An unrecorded portion at the beginning of a roll of magnetic tape that is used solely for threading the tape into the tape recorder/player. The leader is often of a different material than the recorded portion of the tape, stronger and nonmagnetic. 2. A line of dots or dashes that leads the eye from a displayed topic to associated information such as a page number.

leading. (*pronounced ledding*). The space between lines of a printed text. So-called because this spacing was originally produced in typesetting by inserting strips of lead between the lines of type.

leaf. A node in a hierarchy that has no children.

LED. Light-emitting diode. A semiconductor device that emits light when a voltage is applied.

Legendre fractal curve. A fractal curve generated by iterating a Legendre function over the complex plane.

Lempel Ziv Welch. (LZW). A lossless algorithm for data or image compression. Used in the *GIF* file format. See *GIF*.

letterspacing. In typography, the overall amount of white space between characters of a word.

leveling. Changing the amount of detail used in modeling graphics objects as a function of their distance from the observer so that in the final image, all objects appear to have the same amount of detail. This minimizes the computer time spent on modeling details that will not easily be seen.

lexicographic sort. A sort in alphabetical order, but inserting numbers where they would appear if spelled out.

Life game. A game which provides a visual example of the use of cellular automata. The player sets up an array of cells and they then are born, grow, decay, or die according to simple rules. The continually changing cell pattern is displayed on the display screen.

LIFO. Last in, first out. A method of storing data in which the last piece of data to be stored is the first one to be read. Also known as a *stack*.

ligature. In typography, a combination of two letters that frequently occur together and are combined into a single character.

light. 1. Emissions in the frequency band detectable by the human eye. 2. Brightly colored. Having a high color value. Being closer to white than black.

light buffer. A programming technique for efficient computing of shadows. Each point light source is surrounded by a direction cube, and an associated array (which is part of the *light buffer*) contains a list of all objects visible through that cube. The direction of a light ray is first looked up in the *light buffer* and only those objects in the proper directional cube are shadow tested.

light-emitting diode. (LED). A semiconductor device that emits light when a voltage is applied.

light-sensing device. An electronic component that produces a voltage proportional to the light that shines on it.

light source. A source of illumination modeled for use in rendering a graphics image.

light transport. The transfer of light through a medium or from one surface to another.

light valve. A video projector in which a high-powered lamp produces a beam that is scanned in a raster pattern. The beam passes through an optical device that can use an electronic signal to modulate the intensity of the light that passes through it to the screen.

lighting model. The algorithm or equation used to determine the shading of a particular point or surface. Also known as a *shading model* or *illumination model*.

lightness. The brightness of a color as represented in the CIELAB color space. Same as L^*.

line art. An image that is composed entirely of line segments, with no shading, dithering, or halftoning.

line of sight. The direction in which an observer of a scene is looking.

line screen. The resolution of the screen used to produce a halftone from a photograph. It is expressed in lines per inch (lpi) and is usually between 53 lpi and 150 lpi.

line segment. A short straight line. A vector.

line spacing. In typography, the distance from baseline to baseline between two lines of type.

line style. The characteristic of a line as determined by the solid and broken parts of the line; for example, solid lines, dotted lines, dashed lines, center lines, etc.

line width. The thickness of a line drawn on a display.

linear congruential generator. A random number generator which generates numbers using the expression

$$R_{i+1} = \text{mod}(R_i \times s + c, m)$$

where R_{i+1} is the next random number generated, R_i is the seed (or the previous random number), s is a multiplier, c is a constant that is added, and m is the modula number.

linear depth cueing. An image in which the color of an object is interpolated between the object color and the background color as a function of distance.

linear prediction. The prediction of the next value in a series of data based on a linear relationship of the behavior of the preceding pieces of data.

Lipshitz-Holder exponent. A term that is introduced into the equation for a multifractal to assure that the fractal equation does not diverge to 0 or ∞ over the range of iteration.

liquid crystal display. (LCD). A display that consists of a thin layer of a special liquid sandwiched between two glass plates. Application of a voltage through a pair of transparent conductors causes the molecules of the liquid at the affected location to align with the applied field, changing the optical properties of the liquid. A liquid crystal display does not generate light; it must be viewed by reflected light or by backlighting.

Lissajous figure. A figure formed by two mutually perpendicular sinusoidal oscillations. Many different patterns can be created by varying the frequency and phase of the two sinusoids. Stable patterns occur when one sinusoid is an exact multiple of the other.

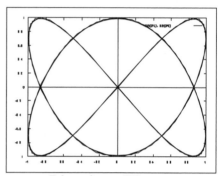

Lissajous Figure

list priority algorithm. An algorithm that assigns priorities to graphics objects in accordance with how they overlap.

lo-res. Low resolution. Low-quality reproduction of image or text.

local area network. (LAN). Computer boards or external boxes, cables, and software used to connect two or more computers so that they have access to each other's resources.

local light source. In rendering a graphics scene, a light source that is near the scene rather than at infinity. For such sources, the light rays do not come from the same direction for every point on an object.

lock height. The distance above a digitizing tablet at which the puck or stylus ceases to function.

lofted surface. A surface created by lofting.

lofting. Determining all of the points on a surface that is defined by a set of cross-section curves through interpolation.

logarithmic space. A space in which the coordinate axes are scaled logarithmically.

logarithmic spiral. A spiral curve generated by the equation

$$r(\phi) = r_0 e^{\gamma\phi}$$

logical. A feature supplied by software rather than built-in as part of the unit hardware.

login. The process used to gain access to a computer bulletin board or operating system.

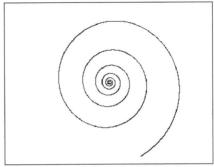

Logarithmic Spiral

logistic parabola. An equation that measures the growth of the next generation of a population from the present generation as follows: $x_{n+1} = rx_n(1-x_n)$. When iterated it gives a fractal bifurcation diagram.

longitude. Angular measurement from a great circle reference circle orthogonal to the equator. The zero reference is the longitude that passes through Greenwich, England. Lines of equal longitude are circles that pass through both the north and south poles. These circles are called *meridians*.

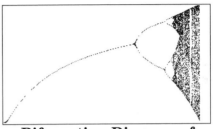

Bifurcation Diagram of Logistic Parabola

look-up table color. A color obtained from a table of permissible colors and used to replace several similar colors in a color quantization process.

Lorentz transformation. A transformation that mixes space and time together.

lossless. Methods of compressing data or images that permit the data to be restored to its original form without any loss of information.

lossy. Methods of compressing data or images that result in the loss of some of the original information.

lpi. Lines per inch.

lpm.   Lines per minute. A measure of the speed at which printers reproduce data.

L-systems.   A language that is used for defining many types of self-similar fractals, including Koch snowflakes and trees.

luminaire.   A light source in a radiosity model.

luminance-color difference space.   The color space used to define colors for television broadcasting. It is a three-dimensional space consisting of a *luminance* value Y, which is a weighted value of the three primary color values red (R), green (G), and blue (B) in the form $Y = 0.30R + 0.59G + 0.11B$. The other two dimensions of the space are defined by the $(B - Y)$ and the $(R - Y)$ differences, either of which can produce a good gray-scale picture by itself.

luminance meter.   An instrument for measuring the luminance of light.

lux.   A measure of luminous flux intensity equal to 1 lumen per square meter or 10.76 footcandles.

LZW.   Lempel Ziv Welch. A lossless algorithm for data or image compression. Used in the *GIF* file format. See *GIF*.

M

M. *mega-*. 1. When applied to computer storage, 1,0248,576 (=2^{20}). 2. When applied to money, 1,000,000 (=10^6).

M2. An analog technique for recording video images.

Mac. Short for the Macintosh™ personal computer. The Macintosh is characterized by a graphical user interface that makes it easy for neophytes to use. It is popular for desktop publishing applications.

MAC. File extension used to designate bit-mapped graphics files created by or compatible with *MacPaint*.

mach band effect. A visual illusion caused by the special sensitivity to edgelike discontinuities of the human eye. It occurs when a continuously toned surface is rendered with too few intensity steps. The regions of constant intensity seem to be nonuniformly shaded with the boundaries to adjacent regions producing a line of subjective brightness.

machine readable. Data on disks or tapes in a form that can be read into a computer.

magenta. A purplish color which is one of the primary colors used in subtractive color imaging processes.

magnetic ink. Ink that can be read by a magnetic scanner. Commonly used to print identifying numbers on bank checks.

magnetic ink character recognition. (MICR). A technique in which a scanning device is used to read characters printed with magnetic ink.

magnetic tape. A data storage medium consisting of a thin plastic ribbon coated with a magnetic material, such as iron oxide, upon which pulses are magnetically recorded.

magneto-optic. A data storage medium similar to magnetic tape or disk, but using a magnetic material whose grains are much smaller. The material is recorded by heating the grains with a laser to make them susceptible to recording and then impressing data with a write head while the area is still hot. A laser is used to heat the area for reading. The result is a higher density of recording than with conventional magnetic material.

magnify. To enlarge an image without rotation by scaling the same amount in all coordinates.

mailbox. A means of avoiding redundant calculations in ray tracing by storing intersection results with each object.

majority voting. A rule used in cellular automata in which a cell assumes a new state that matches the state of the majority of its neighboring cells.

management information system. (MIS). A software system that provides data needed for management decisions and permits the user to manipulate these data.

Mandelbrot set. The fractal curve, named for Benoit Mandelbrot. The set is a plot representing the result of iterating the equation

$$z_{n+1} = z_n^2 + c$$

with $z_0 = 0 + i0$ and c varied over the complex plane. Compare with *Julia set*.

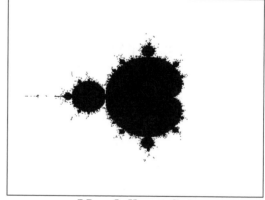

Mandelbrot Set

Manhattan distance. A method of estimating distance that assumes that the sum of the lengths of the three components of a three-dimensional vector is approximately equal to the vector's length.

map. To project a two-dimensional image onto a surface.

margins. In typography, white space surrounding the text area of a page.

marker. A small graphics object that can be moved on a display without changing size. It is used to identify a location where some action is to take place.

Markov source. A source that outputs a one or a zero, with the probability of either being determined by one set of probabilities if the previous output was a one and another set of probabilities if the previous output was a zero.

Markov-Wiener process. A Brownian process with fixed increments.

mask. A pattern of bits which are logically ANDed with incoming data to determine which bits will survive to be further acted upon.

maskable. Capable of having some incoming data bits ignored. Thus color data could be *maskable* so that only a single color (red, for example) would be processed.

mat. An arbitrary size two-dimensional array of real numbers.

matte object. A graphics object rendered in pure black to provide a space for later insertion of another image.

mean time between failures. (MTBF). The mean time between two failures of a piece of equipment. A measure of the reliability of the equipment; the higher the *MTBF*, the greater the reliability.

mean time to repair. (MTTR). The mean time required to repair an equipment failure. This is a measure of the complexity of the equipment; the higher the *MTTR*, the more complex the equipment.

measure. In typography, the length of a typeset line or column width expressed in picas or points.

mechanical. 1. Parts associated with an electronic assembly which perform actions of physical movement. 2. In typography, the completed pasteup for a page.

mechanism. The method by which a graphics-application procedure is implemented.

median. The middle value of a set of values when they are placed in order.

median cut algorithm. A method of quantizing colors which attempts to select K colors to represent an image so that each color represents approximately the same number of pixels.

median filtering. A filtering technique in which the value of a pixel is set to the median of the values of the neighboring pixels.

medical imaging. The application of image processing and display techniques to electronic data from such medical equipment as tomographs or magnetic resonance scanners.

medium. The material upon which information is stored (including magnetic and optical disks, film, etc. Plural *media*.

meg. Slang for megabyte.

megabyte. 1024 kilobytes or 1,048,576 bytes of data.

megaflops. Millions of floating point operations per second. Can be used to define relative measures of computer performance.

member. A named data element that contains part of the state of an instance.

Menelaus's theorem. A theorem that given a triangle and three points, each colinear with one side of the triangle, determines whether the three points are colinear. Useful in curve and surface generation.

Menger sponge. A three-dimensional fractal figure consisting of a cube with a number of square slots removed. It is similar to a *Sierpinski triangle*.

menu. A list of available options on a computer screen, together with software that permits selection of one of these options through movement of a cursor by a mouse or keyboard.

menu-driven. Software in which program options are selected solely thorough moving a cursor to select items from menus, rather than by typing in commands.

Mercator projection. A mapping of a sphere onto a plane so that the longitudes are equally spaced. This results in extensive distortion at high latitudes.

meridian. A line of equal longitude.

Mersenne number. A *Mersenne number* is a number $M_p = 2^p\text{-}1$ where p is a prime.

Mersenne prime. A Mersenne number that is a prime.

mesh. A graphics object that is composed entirely of polygons that have common vertices and edges.

metaball. A surface similar to a *blob* but defined by superimposed piecewise quadratic functions rather than exponentials.

metafile. A file format for graphics storage and transmission that is machine independent. For an example, see *GKS*.

metamer. One of an infinite number of spectra that are perceived as the same color by the human eye.

metameric match. Two or more colors that appear identical to the human eye, even though the actual distribution of wavelengths may be different for each color.

method. A named operation on an instance.

mickey. A unit of mouse movement. It is usually 1/200th of an inch.

MICR. Magnetic ink character recognition. A technique in which a scanning device is used to read characters printed with magnetic ink.

microfacet. A surface facet assumed for theoretical purposes whose scale is that of the roughness of a surface. Assumed distributions of *microfacets* are used in some models of surface reflectance.

microfiche. A 4" × 6" sheet of film containing highly reduced images of approximately 270 pages of a document together with a title that can be read without magnification.

microfilm. A roll of 35-mm film on which are recorded reduced images of document pages in sequence.

midpoint. The point halfway between the two ends of a line.

midpoint displacement method, midpoint subdivision, or **midpoint recursion.** A technique for drawing fractal mountains that starts with one or more large triangles and recursively subdivides each triangle into four smaller triangles by drawing lines between the midpoints of the triangle sides.

millilambert. A unit of luminance that is equal to 0.3142 nit.

minify. To reduce an image in size (often by a power of 2) by replacing a square group of pixels with a single pixel that has the average color of the group.

Minkowski-Bouligand dimension. A dimension greater than the Euclidian dimension which is the proper alternative to the Hausdorff-Besikovitch dimension in expressing the dimensional characteristics of some fractal curves.

minus leading. In typography, leading in which the distance from baseline to baseline between two lines of type is less than the type size.

MIPS. Millions of instructions per second. A measure of the speed of a computer.

mirror image. An image in which the original right and left are reversed, but top and bottom remain the same.

mirroring. A capability in a drawing program for automatically copying an existing graphics object at another location and reflected symmetrically about a prescribed line.

MIS. Management information system. A software system that provides data needed for management decisions and permits the user to manipulate these data.

misconvergence. The alignment error of the red, green, and blue guns of a cathode-ray tube measured as a mean distance between centers of color spot pairs.

Misiurewicz point. A value of c on the Mandelbrot set for which the point $z=0$ is preperiodic but not periodic and is eventually drawn into a repulsive circle.

Mitchell filter. A filter used in image rescaling.

mitre. A method of treating the ends of thick lines that join to create a proper joint.

model. In graphics, a collection of graphics objects that represent a scene or a more complex object.

modeling. Activities that construct a graphics data base without any attempt to render the scene.

modem. Modulator-demodulator. A device for transmitting and receiving digital signals over telephone lines.

Moebius strip. A surface that has only one side. A model can be made by taking a strip of paper, giving one end a 180-degree twist, and then gluing the ends together.

moire. Undesirable global beat patterns produced by overlaying dot patterns (such as halftone representations of photographs) that have fine detail of approximately the same scale.

molecular modeling. The use of computer graphics to model atoms and molecules and determine the interaction of their structures.

monochromatic light. Light that contains photons of only a single frequency.

monochromatic triples. A set of the three primary colors that are all of the same value, for example *(0.6, 0.6, 0.6)*. *Monochromatic triples* always produce shades of gray.

monochromic. 1. In reference to display cathode-ray tubes, having a single phosphor, thereby producing only a single color display such as white, green, or amber. 2. In reference to light, having a single frequency, as can occur in a laser light beam.

monohedral tiling. The repeated use of a single geometric figure (with different orientations, if necessary) to completely fill a plane.

monospacing. Spacing technique used by some printers, in which every character occupies the same amount of space regardless of its relative width.

morphing. The process of converting one image to another by warping the original image to some intermediate distorted shape and then warping this distorted shape back to the second image over the course of a number of animation frames.

motherboard. The main printed circuit board of a computer, having the principal circuitry upon it and having connectors for attaching *daughter boards*.

Motif. A graphic user interface developed as a proposed standard by the Open Software Foundation.

motion blur. The deliberate blurring of the edges of an object in an image to give the illusion of motion. Blurring is not a characteristic of motion itself, but occurs because of the slow speed of photographic shutters.

MOTIVE. A CADDS tool for analyzing how the layout of a printed circuit board will affect the timing of various signals on it.

mottle. Gross variations in the intensity of a printed image that were not intended or desired.

mouse. A computer hardware device in which the user moves the device over a surface, causing a ball to roll and move the cursor on a display.

MR scanner. Magnetic resonance scanner. A device that measures the magnetic resonance characteristics of spinning atoms to produce images.

MS-DOS. The basic operating system used by IBM PC personal computers and PC clones.

MSP. A file extension used to designate bit-mapped image files produced in a format compatible with *Microsoft Paint* program.

MTBF. Mean time between failures. The mean time between two failures of a piece of equipment. A measure of the reliability of the equipment; the higher the *MTBF*, the greater the reliability.

MTTR. Mean time to repair. The mean time required to repair an equipment failure. This is a measure of the complexity of the equipment; the higher the *MTTR*, the more complex the equipment.

multifractal Julia set. The Julia set of a rational function which has more than two attractors.

multimedia. The use of a number of media in disseminating information. For example, text, audio, graphics, motion pictures, etc., can all be used together to produce an overall effect.

multisync monitor. A monitor that can automatically synchronize to several horizontal and vertical frequencies so that a number of different resolutions can be produced on the screen.

Munsell color system. A system using cylindrical coordinates to specify color values. The *hue* of the color is specified as an angle, the *chroma* by radial distance, and the *value* (dark to light) by distance along the z axis.

N

NAND. Normally written in all capital letters, although not an acronym, to indicate a logic function. 1. A logic function that is the opposite of AND (not AND). For every bit of one of two inputs that is a zero, the corresponding bit of the output is a one. 2. To perform the NAND operation.

NAPLIPS.   North American presentation level protocol. A standard object-oriented graphics ASCII-character file format.

National Television Standards Committee. (NTSC). 1. The organization for setting television standards. 2. The standard for color television in the United States, Japan, and parts of South America.

NCGA.   National Computer Graphics Association. An organization for those interested in computer graphics.

near letter quality. (NLQ). Output from a printer that is almost as good as typewriter output.

negative. A photographic image in which the tone values are reversed. Black tones are white on the negative, white tones are black, etc. When light is projected through a negative onto photosensitive film or paper, a positive image is produced.

negative light.   A light source whose color is defined in negative numbers. An artificial construct used when rendering a scene to make an object surface darker without modifying all the existing light sources.

nested face.   A polygon that is coplanar with another polygon, from which it inherits some attributes.

nesting.   A hierarchical file structure consisting, for example, of directories, subdirectories, subsubdirectories, etc.

network. Two or more computers, electronically connected so that they may share each other's resources.

Newell's method.   A way of computing the plane equation of an arbitrary 3-D polygon.

Newman and Sproul.   One of the classic texts on computer graphics. *Principles of Interactive Computer Graphics*   by William Newman and Robert Sproull.

Newton's method.   A method for solving an equation that begins by making a guess z_0 as to a root of the equation   and then iterating the equation

$$z_{n+1} = z_n - \frac{f(z_n)}{f'(z_n)}$$

At each iteration the result comes closer to the actual value of a root.

Newton's method fractal.   A fractal created by mapping the solution of an equation by Newton's method for every starting point within the complex plane.

nibble.   Four binary bits, or half a byte. Sometimes spelled *nybble*.

nit.   A unit of luminance. The photometric brightness of a surface equal to a candela per square meter or to 0.2919 footlamberts.

NLQ.   Near letter quality. Output from a printer that is almost as good as typewriter output.

node.   1. A connection point on a network. 2. An entry in a hierarchy.

noise.   A signal whose amplitude varies randomly with time.

noise, 1/f.   A completely random amplitude signal whose power is inverse to frequency. Also known as *pink noise*.

nolid.   An Archimedean solid having fourteen faces that consist of squares or triangles. Also known as a *cuboctahedron*.

nonimpact printer. A printer that uses a technique that does not require mechanical devices to strike the paper.

noninterfaced. A display where each line is written in sequence and all lines are refreshed for each vertical scan.

nonlinear mapping. Transformation of an image from one surface to another with variations in scale or rotation that change the shape of the final image.

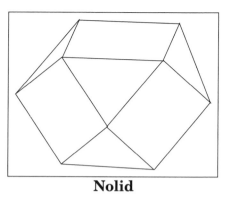

Nolid

nonlocality tension. A parameter used in *interPhong shading* to help determine whether the shading should be closer to *faceted* or *Phong shading*.

nonuniform. Having subdivisions that are not equally spaced.

nonuniform rational B-spline. (NURB). A mathematical description of a curved surface in which the surface is specified as a ratio of two polynomials for each region of the spline.

NOR. Normally written in all capital letters, although not an acronym, to indicate a logic function. 1. A logic function that is the opposite of OR (not OR). For every bit where either one of two inputs is a one, the corresponding bit of the output is a zero. 2. To perform the NOR operation.

normal. 1. Perpendicular to a surface. 2. A unit vector that is perpendicular to a surface at a designated point.

normalized. 1. Scaled to a designated range or value. 2. A *normalized* vector is a vector that is scaled so that its length is one. Also known as a *unit vector*.

North American presentation level protocol. (NAPLPS). A standard object-oriented graphics ASCII-character file format.

NTSC. National Television Standards Committee. 1. The organization for setting television standards. 2. The standard for color television in the United States, Japan, and parts of South America.

NTSC encoder. An electronic circuit that converts an RGB video signal and associated sync signals to an NTSC-compatible composite video signal.

NURB. Nonuniform rational B-spline. A mathematical description of a curved surface in which the surface is specified as a ratio of two polynomials for each region of the spline.

nybble. Four binary bits, or half a byte. Sometimes spelled *nibble*.

Nyquist limit. The highest frequency in an electronic signal that may be reliably sampled for a given sampling rate. The theoretical limit is one-half the sampling rate.

O

object. 1. A primitive graphics geometric figure. 2. A collection of related data that may be operated upon by a particular set of functions.

object buffer. A ray-tracing technique that first renders an image by storing the object number of the nearest intersected object for each ray in a frame buffer. For each pixel, the color of the object at the intersection is then determined.

object oriented. 1. Graphics operations that deal directly with primitive geometric figures rather than bit-mapped representations. 2. A style of computer programming in which collections of related data are formed into objects that are operated upon by sending and receiving messages to the objects.

object-oriented programming. A programming technique based upon objects that consist of data structures which associates these with operations upon them.

object space. The particular coordinate system which is used to define a graphics object.

occlusion. That part of graphics image processing that deals with the fact that objects nearer to an observer cover those that are farther away. Also called *occultation*.

occlusion mask. A pattern of bits that consists of selected samples from an array covering a pixel. Used in antialiasing to determine how much of a pixel is on a specified surface.

occultation. That part of graphics image processing that deals with the fact that objects nearer to an observer cover those that are farther away. Also called *occlusion*.

OCR. Optical character recognition. Any method used for converting scanned text images into computer-recognizable text characters.

octahedron. An eight-sided solid.

octal. A number system to the base eight. Octal numbers can be converted to binary by writing each octal digit as a pattern of three bits.

octant. One of eight divisions of a plane produced by drawing lines starting with the x axis and then at 45-degree angles around the circle.

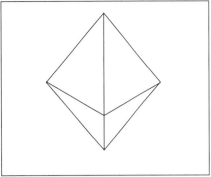

Octahedron

octet. An eight-bit byte.

octree. A tree-like subdivision of three-dimensional space created by recursively subdividing a cube into eight equal sized smaller cubes, down to the smallest size cubes desired. At the lowest level of subdivision, the elements are known as *voxels*. For any particular subdivision cube, it is possible to stop the subdivision process without going further. Thus an *octree* could be created where subdivision stopped when each subdivided cube contained precisely one primitive graphics object.

OEM. Original equipment manufacturer. The original maker of equipment marketed by and under the name of another vender.

off-line. 1. Not presently available for use by the computer system. 2. Operations on data that are performed apart from the computer system in which it is to be used.

omnifont. Character recognition system that can recognize any font without having to relearn its characteristics.

on-line. Available for use by the computer system.

one-sided surface. A surface that is rendered when one side faces the observer and omitted when the other side faces the observer.

open. A graphics object that has a surface which may be viewed from either side, depending upon the viewpoint.

open system. A computer system in which the details of system architecture and input and output hardware and software interfaces are made available to outside developers.

optical character recognition. (OCR). Use of a combination of software with a scanner to capture and recognize text characters on a printed page and convert them into machine-readable data.

optical disk. A storage device that is written to and read by a laser light beam. Some optical disks are known as WORM (write once read many) disks because a given part of the surface can only be written once and is then not erasable. However, it can be read as many times as desired.

optical scanner. A device that scans pages of human-readable text and converts them to machine-readable digital data.

optical storage. The storing of data on laser or CD-ROM disks.

optics. The branch of physics that studies the behavior of light.

optimization. The modification of a software package to make it as efficient as possible.

OR. Normally written in all capital letters, although not an acronym, to indicate a logic function. 1. A logic function in which for every bit of any of two or more inputs that is a one, the corresponding bit of the output is a one. 2. To perform the OR operation.

orbit. The path of a point when a transformation is recursively applied.

ordered dithering. A technique for reducing high-precision, two-dimensional information to lower precision, while retaining as much information as possible through the use of positional information.

ordinate. The vertical or y component of a two-dimensional coordinate system. The horizontal or x component is the *abscissa*.

orientation. The relative direction of text or images on a printed page. If the text is oriented horizontally, this is called *landscape* orientation. If the text is oriented vertically, it is called *portrait* orientation. These terms originated from the way in which landscape and portrait pictures are usually oriented in photographs.

original equipment manufacturer. (OEM). The original maker of equipment marketed by and under the name of another vender.

ornament. A small stylized piece of artwork included with text for decoration.

orphan. A word or short line of text ending a paragraph which is carried over to the beginning of the next page.

orthographic projection. A projection from three dimensions to two dimensions that does not make any provision for perspective so that object sizes do not change regardless of their distance from the observer.

OS-2. IBM's operating system for personal computers.

outline font. A type font in which the characters are formed by curves rather that being bit-mapped. This permits scaling of the type to any desired size and also permits character rotation.

output device. A device such as a monitor or printer that presents computer information to the outside world.

overcoat. A layer of transparent plastic that protects optical recording media from damage by dust and scratches.

overhead. Transmitted or stored data that are not part of the actual text. It is used for control, addressing, error checking and recovery, etc.

overlay. 1. A graphics image that is superimposed on another graphics image. 2. A portion of a computer program that is only loaded into memory when a kernel program calls for its execution.

overlay planes. Additional memory planes that permit storage of an overlay image so that it may be displayed temporarily without destroying the underlying main image.

overloaded function or **overload operator.** In C++, a function, such as +, that is redefined for a different class of object.

oversampling. Reducing aliasing artifacts by computing the color of a number of sample points within a pixel and taking a weighted average of the samples as the pixel color. Also called *supersampling*.

overscan. A part of a displayed image that cannot be seen because the display scan extends beyond the borders of the display device.

P

pack. To compress data.

packet. A group of bits consisting of control information, data, and error correction bits, packaged together for transmission purposes.

packet exchange. (PEX). A message communication service used in the Xerox Network Systems (XNS) architecture.

page description language. A specialized computer language that describes the appearance of a printed page. Typically includes descriptions of the type fonts used, instructions for margins, spacing, other layout information, and the text and graphics to appear on the page. Printers or electronic typesetters designed to work with a *page description language* include a processor that converts the language to an actual page layout, which is then printed.

page printer. A printer that prints an entire page at a time instead of printing character by character or line by line.

paginate. In typography, to number the pages of a book sequentially.

paint. An operation in graphics creating software in which the mouse is used to create a line on the screen as it is moved. The user may select the characteristics (such as width and texture) of the "brush" that is used to *paint*.

paint program. A computer program that creates raster images in color by using the mouse to draw lines and create simple geometric figures directly on the screen. The final image is stored in a file in bit-mapped form.

painter's algorithm. A method of coping with the problem of hidden surfaces by rendering objects in the reverse order of their distance from the observer (farther objects first; closer objects last). All surfaces are rendered; those that are hidden in the final picture are simply painted over.

PAL. 1. Phase alternate line. The standard for color television in most of the world except France, United States, and Japan. 2. Programmable array logic. An integrated circuit that contains an array of logic gates that can be permanently programmed for a particular purpose.

pale. A color having very low color saturation so that it appears almost white.

palette. The colors that may be displayed at any one time by a computer color monitor. Colors are limited primarily by the amount of memory in the video adapter board that is used to store video information. Typically color modes allow 16 colors to be displayed out of 64 available and 256 to be displayed out of 16 million available.

palette animation. A method of simulating animation in which the palette of colors used for the scene is changed from one frame to the next to give the appearance of motion.

Palo Alto Research Center. (PARC). A research center for Xerox Corp. which has made significant contributions to the development of graphics user interfaces.

pan. To change the image that is being viewed to a portion of the overall picture that is currently not on the screen.

pancake window. An optical device that is placed in front of the cathode-ray tube in flight simulators to make the displayed image appear more distant.

pantone matching system. (PMS). A method of describing colors in which each color is assigned a number.

parabola. A curve that is the locus of a point that moves in such a way that its undirected distances from a fixed point and a fixed line are equal. Its equation is

$$y^2 = 2px \quad or \quad x^2 = 2py$$

parallel. Transmission of bits over a set of parallel wires with one wire devoted to each bit that is to be transmitted simultaneously. Commonly used to send the 8 bits that make up one ASCII character simultaneously to a printer.

parallel connected stripes. (PCS). A hierarchical data structure used to store graphics object data.

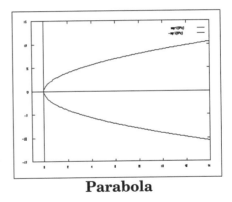

Parabola

parallel projection. A technique for converting a three-dimensional scene into two dimensions. A projection plane is placed in front of the scene and parallel to its coordinate system. A center of projection is selected by projecting a line from the center of the scene through the center of the projection plane and selecting a point on this line somewhere in front of the projection plane. Each line or surface of the scene is then projected on the projection screen by drawing a line from it to the center of projection and marking where this line intersects the projection screen.

parametric. The equation for a curve or surface that is defined in terms of some intermediate variables rather than directly in terms of coordinate values.

PARC. Palo Alto Research Center. A research center for Xerox Corp. which has made significant contributions to the development of graphics user interfaces.

parcel. A collection of primitive graphics objects that have been preprocessed so that they can be rendered efficiently with any desired viewpoint.

parent. A node in a hierarchy that is higher than another node.

parity. An additional bit that is added to a block of data for error detection. For odd parity, the number of bits in the block (including the parity bit) that are 1's is odd; for even parity, the number of bits in the block (including the parity bit) that are 1's is even. If the number is not odd or even, as required for the type parity, the computer knows that the block contains an error, but doesn't know which bit is in error.

partial kd tree. Partial k-dimensional tree. A binary subdivision of k-dimensional space, one dimension at a time, in which empty subdivisions are not represented.

particle system. A computer graphics technique, originated by W. Reeves, which represents irregular objects, such as smoke, clouds, or water, as a collection of particles that are varying in time. Stochastic processes are used to create, move, and remove particles so as to control the overall shape and texture of the object.

partitioning. Subdividing a space into a number of smaller spaces or cells.

patch. 1. A small simple curved surface that is combined with other *patches* to create a complex surface. 2. A correction inserted in a software program to correct an error without extensive rewriting of the program.

patch cracking. Cracking that occurs when a surface is subdivided into patches and then the patches are redrawn to approximate the original surface. It occurs because the edges of adjacent patches are not identically described due to computer round-off errors. See *cracking*.

patch visibility index. A number associated with a vertex that measures the potential occlusion.

path tracing. Following the path of a ray backwards from the eye.

pattern mask. A matrix of threshold values that is used to determine which of two adjacent output gray-scale values will be assigned to a pixel.

pattern matching. A technique for optical character reading. The software contains a template of each possible character. When the scanner reads a character, it is compared with the templates until a match is found and then reports the resulting ASCII equivalent.

PC. Short for personal computer. Usually used to refer to the IBM personal computer or a clone.

PCB. Printed circuit board. A plastic board originally coated with copper on one or both sides. The copper coating is etched to create a pattern of wire connections. Holes are then drilled for mounting electronic components to the board.

PCL. Printer control language. A common page description language for laser printers developed by Hewlett-Packard.

PCM. Pulse code modulation. A technique for digitizing analog signals in which a train of pulses forms a digital representation of the analog level.

PCS. Parallel connected stripes. A hierarchical data structure used to store graphics object data.

PCX. A file format using run-length encoding to store bit-mapped graphics in compressed form. Originated by Z-Soft Corp and first used in the *PC Paintbrush* program.

Peano curve. A space-filling fractal curve obtained by repeatedly replacing the middle third of each line segment by a pattern of six line segments that are one-third of the length of the original line segment, causing a square to be formed at the left and right of the middle third of the original line segment.

pedestal level. The voltage level of a video signal that totally suppresses the electron beam of the cathode-ray tube during blanking. Also known as *blanking level*.

pel. A single element of a discrete display. Also known as a *pixel*.

pen plotter. A plotter in which one or more pens are electronically moved to trace the data on a sheet of paper.

pen-based computing. A computer system that makes use of an electronic pen or stylus to provide data input.

penetron. A type of color cathode-ray tube in which layers of red and green phosphors are applied to the interior of the faceplate in such a way that the color of the display depends upon the amount that the electron beam penetrates the phosphor layers, which in turn depends upon the electron beam accelerating voltage. It provides simpler and higher resolution displays than color-mask tubes, but cannot produce shades of blue. Also known as a *beam penetration display*.

Penrose tiling. The tiling of a plane with only two different tiles.

penumbra. That portion of a shadow where part, but not all, of an extended light source is occluded by a shadowing object.

period doubling. A phenomenon in fractal attractors in which, at a certain critical value, the attractor splits in two.

periodic orbit. The path followed by a point when a set of values is calculated using a recursion equation.

periodic plane tesselation. The complete tiling of a plane by repetition of the same shape.

peripheral vision. Vision from the edges of the eye, where distribution of rods exceeds that of cones. It is characterized by lower resolution, less color perception, higher sensitivity to motion, and higher sensitivity to light.

Perlin noise function. A function that varies randomly between -1 and +1 throughout three-dimensional space with an autocorrelation distance of about 1 in every direction. Also known as the *random noise function*.

persistence. The capability of a cathode-ray tube phosphor to continue to emit light for a time after the exciting stream of electrons is removed. Phosphors that have long persistence glow for a long time after the beam is removed. This reduces objectionable flicker but causes blurring of fast moving data. Phosphors with short persistence glow for only a very short time after the beam is removed. They are capable of displaying fast moving action without blur, but need to be refreshed more often to avoid flicker.

perspective. The apparent reduction in size of objects in proportion to their distance from the observer when viewed in three-dimensional space.

perspective projection. The mathematical transformation of three-dimensional objects into two dimensions by dividing the x and y lengths of the object by z (the distance from the observer) to give the illusion of depth.

PET scanner. Positron emission tomography scanner. An electronic device that produces the images of inner body parts for medical purposes.

PEX.   1. PHIGS extension to X. A protocol for a three-dimensional extension to X11 based on PHIGS+. 2. Packet exchange. A message communication service used in the Xerox Network Systems (XNS) architecture.

PGL.   File extension used to designate the Hewlett-Packard graphics language format.

Pharaoh's breastplate.   A fractal curve produced through the use of inversion.

phase alternate line.   (PAL). The standard for color television in most of the world except France, United States, and Japan.

phase change recording.   An optical data recording technique in which data are recorded by causing a laser beam to strike the recording medium and cause it to crystalize. The medium is read by reading it with a laser beam that only reflects from the crystallized areas.

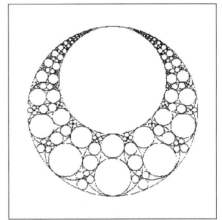

Pharaoh's Breastplate

phase space.   A space in which all of the characteristics of a dynamical system at an instant in time are collapsed into a single point. As time is varied, the picture shows the complete behavior of the system over a time interval.

PHIGS.   Programmers hierarchical interface for graphics systems. A software interface standard for graphics that includes data structures for high-level three-dimensional applications.

PHIGS extension to X.   (PEX). A protocol for a three-dimensional extension to X11 based on PHIGS+.

PHIGS+.   An extension to the original PHIGS specification that includes more extensive lighting models.

Phong illumination or **Phong shading.**   A technique for rendering the highlights that appear on glossy surfaces by taking the cosine of the angle between the incident light on the surface and the viewing direction vector and raising it to a predetermined power. The diffused light is then increased by this factor. Originated by Phong Bui Tong in 1975.

phosphor. A chemical substance, such as that used on the back of a cathode-ray tube face, which emits light when struck by a beam of electrons.

phot. A unit of illuminance equal to 0.0001 lux.

photorealistic rendering. Techniques for rendering an image so that it appears as realistic as a photograph.

photochromic. A compound that becomes dark when exposed to light.

photocomposition. The printing of information by using photographic means to produce characters and graphics on a light-sensitive paper or film which is then used as a master for the printing process.

photoinversion. The transformation of a gray-scale computer graphics image by replacing each pixel with its gray-scale opposite. This same process in photography consists of making a positive print from a negative.

photomapping. The mapping of a photographic image onto a surface.

photometer. A device that measures luminance and reports the results in units weighted to match the spectral intensity of the human visual system.

photometric. Relating to light measurements weighted for the properties of the human visual system.

photon. An imaginary particle of light.

photo-optic memory. An optical data storage technique wherein a laser is used to record data on light-sensitive film.

photopic. Relating to vision principally by the cones of the human eye, characterized by bright light and color sensitivity.

photopic luminous efficiency function. A function of the wavelength of light that specifies the relative sensitivity of the human visual system under high brightness conditions.

photoplotter. A high-accuracy, high-definition plotter that plots with a beam of light on photosensitive material.

photosensor. A light-sensitive reading device employed in optical scanners.

phototypesetter. A device that uses photographic means to produce character images on a light-sensitive paper or film to create a master for use in a printing process.

pi. 1. In typography, jumbled type that needs to be sorted into the proper bins of a type case before reuse. 2. In mathematics, the ratio of the circumference of a circle to its diameter.

pi character. In typography, a nonalphanumeric symbol that has the same size as a letter or number such as a smiling face. Type fonts consisting entirely of *pi characters* are available. Using such a font, each letter or number of a standard keyboard will cause an associated *pi character* to be printed. Also known as a *dingbat*.

PIC. A file extension designating a compressed bit-map image format compatible with the *PC Paint Plus* painting program.

pica. A unit of measurement used in typography and desktop publishing. One pica is equal to 12 points or 1/6 inch.

pick aperture. The area in which the cursor must be placed to select a desired action.

pick-highlight cycle. The modifying of a particular object's color or appearance on the display to indicate that it has been selected by the cursor.

pick identifier. See *picking*.

picking. The process in which a user moves a cursor on a display to a particular area in order to select an application that the computer is to perform. The software actions needed to perform this are first that the program identify the cursor location coordinates, second that it compare them with a table of location areas versus numbers called the *pick identifiers*, and third that it perform a set of functions identified with the selected number.

PICT. A file extension used to designate object-oriented graphics files compatible with many Apple Macintosh graphics programs.

pie chart. A graph in which a circle represents the whole and is divided into proportionally sized segments, each representing the part of the whole having some characteristic.

pinch roller. A rubber wheel that presses a magnetic tape against the capstan with constant pressure to assure that the tape speed remains constant during reading and writing.

pincushioning. Distortion of the image on a video screen in which the middle of the top, bottom, and sides of the display are pushed in.

pinhole camera. The simplest form of camera, consisting of a box with a pinhole in the center of one wall and a sheet of film on the inside of the other wall. As long as the pinhole is small enough, it acts as a good-quality lens of very small aperture.

pink noise. A completely random amplitude signal whose power is inverse to frequency. Also known as *1/f noise*.

pit. A laser-created indentation in an optical disk that represents a bit of data.

pitch. 1. The number of characters per inch in a line of text, measured horizontally. This number is meaningful only for fixed spacing fonts, since proportional fonts have a different *pitch* for every character. 2. The angular displacement of an object about the *x* axis in the *x-y* plane.

pixel. A single element of a discrete display. Also known as a *pel*.

pixellization. A special video effect in which an image is divided into a grid containing squares that are treated as oversized pixels, with each assigned a color derived from the original image color in the area.

pixmap. In the X Window system, a two-dimensional array of graphics data in which each pixel of a display has its color represented by at least one bit.

Pixrect. A low-level two-dimensional graphics program by Sun Microsystems for Sun workstations.

Pixwin. A program used in the implementation of the Sun-Windows window system.

PKZIP. A popular program for compressing computer files using the Lempel Ziv Welch compression algorithm. Files compressed with this program have the extension *.ZIP*. Designed and destributed by PKWare Co.

PKUNZIP. A program for decompressing files that have been compressed with *PKZIP*. Such files have the extension *.ZIP*. Designed and destributed by PKWare Co.

planar. Contained within a plane. Having two dimensions.

planar cubic curve. A curve defined by a cubic equation and confined to a plane.

plane. A two-dimensional surface of infinite extent.

plane equations. Equations that define lines, points, or curves on a plane.

plasma display. A flat display screen consisting of a gas sandwiched between two glass plates. A grid of horizontal and vertical wires associated with the display causes the gas to glow at the intersection of the particular pair of horizontal and vertical wires that are activated by application of a voltage.

plot. To create an image by drawing straight line segments.

Plot3D. A program for displaying scientific data in graphics form. Originated by NASA. Often used to display fluid dynamics data. Also applied to the file format used for storing such graphics images.

plotter. A device that creates images by drawing lines on paper.

PMS. Pantone matching system. A method of describing colors in which each color is assigned a number.

point. 1. A unit of measurement in typography or desktop publishing. One point is 1/72 of an inch. 2. A location in space specified by a set of coordinate values.

point and shoot interface. A graphics user interface (GUI) featuring icons that are selected by moving a cursor on the display with a mouse.

point light source. A light source that radiates from a single point in space.

point-on-line test. Any method for determining whether a given point is on a specified line.

point sampling. The process of determining pixel color by sampling a point on the image that is within the pixel bounds.

point size. In typography, the size of type measured from the top of the ascender to the bottom of the descender.

pointer. An input device that controls cursor position in the X Window system.

pointing device. A piece of hardware used to input position data to a computer that is used to move the position of a cursor on the display screen. Examples are *mice* and *track balls*.

polling. A technique for data transfer on a computer network in which a network server interrogates the other computers periodically to determine when one of them has data ready to transfer.

polygon. A two-dimensional figure consisting of an ordered set of vertices connected in sequence by sides that do not intersect, so as to form a closed surface. A polygon may be tessellated into triangles. See *concave polygon* and *convex polygon*.

polygon, generalized. A graphics figure, not necessarily coplanar, consisting of an ordered set of vertices connected in sequence by sides that may intersect, so as to form a closed surface. It may not be possible to tessellate a *generalized polygon* into triangles.

polygon table. A table of data used in scan conversion which contains the coefficients of the plane equation, shading or color information, and an in-out Boolean flag for each polygon that is part of the image that is being scan converted.

polygonal pens. A method of drawing wide lines using polygons defined by integer offset vectors, discovered by Hobby.

polyhedron. A closed three-dimensional object comprised of polygons, where each edge of a polygon is shared with another polygon and each vertex is shared by two or more polygons.

polyline. A set of contiguous straight line segments that approximates a curve.

polymarker. A graphics object that is defined by a marker and a list of marker locations.

polymorphism. A characteristic of object-oriented programming in which a given name may refer to an object of any one of a number of related classes that may respond to a given operation in different ways.

popularity algorithm. A method of quantizing colors in which the new, limited range of colors consists of the K colors most frequently occurring in the image.

port. A computer channel that interfaces with an input or output device.

portrait. Orientation of a page such that text is in readable direction when the page length exceeds the page width.

positive. A photographic film or print that accurately represents the original tone value (that is, original blacks are black in the print and original whites are white). Contrast this with *negative*.

positron emission tomography scanner. (PET scanner). An electronic device that produces the images of inner body parts for medical purposes.

postconcatenation. A modification of transformation matrices that permits the transformation process to be performed much faster on a computer.

posterization. Reducing the number of colors or shades of gray in an image so that boundaries between different colors or shades of gray are obvious, with no blending effects. Used to give an artistic effect.

PostScript. (trademark of Adobe systems). A language that represents fonts, text, and graphics so that a printer that understands the language can use the language description to produce a printed page.

potentially visible. A graphics object that may be partially or completely occluded and therefore requires further processing.

prediction-correction coding. An image data file compression technique that makes a prediction based on past history to estimate the current value of a datum and then generates a correction term to correct any error.

premastering. The process whereby data files are converted into a compact disk format for producing CD-ROMs. A 288-byte error correction block is added to every 2048-byte user block.

Prewitt operators. A pair of 3×3 matrices used to sharpen the edges of objects in an image.

primitive. A graphics object for which processing is included in a graphics or rendering program. *Primitives* may be rendered directly or combined to create more complex graphics objects.

print screen. A computer command that causes the data on the monitor display screen to be printed out by the printer.

print spooler. A memory buffer devoted to the printer and the software needed to transfer data being printed to this memory. This frees up the computer for other use while the printer loads and prints directly from the memory buffer.

printed circuit board. (PCB). A plastic board originally coated with copper on one or both sides. The copper coating is etched to create a pattern of wire connections. Holes are then drilled for mounting electronic components to the board.

printer control language. (PCL). A common page description language for laser printers developed by Hewlett-Packard.

prioritization. The sorting of graphics objects according to their closeness to the observer.

priority ordered. Graphics objects listed in order from near to far for occlusion processing that takes place during rendering of a graphics image.

procedural surface. A graphics surface that is implicitly defined for modeling by specifying the equation of a curve or solid, by giving the expression for sweeping such a curve or solid through space, or by Boolean intersections of simpler solids using constructive solid geometry.

process color printing. The production of a full-color image on paper by combining two or more subtractive color inks. The colors used for full-color reproduction are cyan, magenta, yellow, and black.

process separation. Creation of the four negatives used to generate the cyan, magenta, yellow, and black subtractive color images in process color printing.

programmable array logic. (PAL). An integrated circuit that contains an array of logic gates that can be permanently programmed for a particular purpose.

programmable read-only memory. (PROM). Digital memory in which data can be stored permanently by one write operation. Data can be read many times, but cannot be rewritten.

programmers' hierarchical interface for graphics systems. (PHIGS). A software interface standard for graphics that includes data structures for high-level three-dimensional applications.

projection. The mapping of the surface of a three-dimensional object onto another, differently shaped surface, or vice versa.

PROM. Programmable read-only memory. Digital memory in which data can be stored permanently by one write operation. Data can be read many times, but cannot be rewritten.

propagated light. Light that arrives at a surface and is then subsequently transmitted again in some way.

proportional spacing. The use of a special appropriate width in printing each character of a font.

prototile. A small geometric figure used repeatedly to fill a plane.

proximity search. A search in which two words can be specified together with the maximum number of words that may occur between them and every situation that meets this specification is detected.

proximity testing. A method of reducing a color image to fourteen colors by finding the face of a cuboctahedron that is nearest to the coordinates of the point in three-dimensional space that defines the original color.

pseudocolor. A color that results from pseudocoloring.

pseudocoloring. Use of a color table to assign colors other than the natural object colors to an image.

pseudorandom number. A number generated by an algorithm that produces a series of numbers that have all of the characteristics of random numbers except that the set is periodic with a very large period.

puck. An input device similar to a mouse but with a number of additional special-purpose pushbuttons. It is used in creating computer graphics.

pulse code modulation. The modulation of a carrier with pulses whose presence at a given position represents the existence of a one in a binary number. The series of binary numbers often represents samples of an analog signal.

pure. 1. Appearing saturated in color. 2. A monochromatic (single-frequency) color, as produced by a laser beam.

purity. The degree to which a uniformly colored region is correctly displayed, particularly on a shadow-mask cathode-ray tube.

Purkinje effect. The change in color perception for low light levels as the eye adjusts from day (scoptic) vision (using primarily the cones as receptors) to night (photopic) vision (using primarily the rods as receptors). Reds and oranges appear to lose brightness relative to blues and greens.

pyramid. A solid having five faces; a square base and four triangle sides.

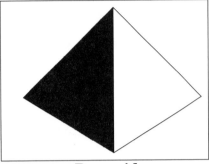

Pyramid

Q

Q. The green-to-magenta component of a color represented in the YIQ color coordinate space. It is the quadrature component in a composite color television signal.

QBF. The message *The quick brown fox jumped over the lazy dog* which is used for testing printers and displays, since it contains every letter of the alphabet.

QE. Quality engineering. The processes whereby the quality of a designed and/or manufactured product is assured.

quad. Also known as a *quadrilateral*. A graphics figure that is defined by four vertices connected by line segments.

quad, concave. A quad in which it is possible to draw a line between two vertices that does not pass entirely through the quad.

quad, convex. A quad in which every line segment connecting two vertices is entirely within the quad.

quad, generalized. Any quad, including ones that are self-intersecting or nonplanar.

quad tessellation. The subdivision of a quad into two triangles.

quadrant. In two-dimensional geometry, one of the four quarters into which the plane is divided by the orthogonal x and y axes of the cartesian coordinate system.

quadratic blending. The interpolation between two colors by using the function $N(t) = (1 - t)^2 N_1 + t^2 N_2$.

quadratic spline. A curve used as an antialiasing filter function to reconstruct an image. It has the equation

$$g(r) = \begin{cases} 1 - \dfrac{r^2}{st}, & 0 \le r \le s \\[2ex] \dfrac{(t-r)^2}{t(t-s)}, & s \le r \le t \\[2ex] 0, & t \ge r \end{cases}$$

quadratic surface equation. The general implicit equation for a quadric surface. When expressed as a 4 × 4 matrix it is said to be in the quadric form.

quadric Koch island. One of the Koch family of fractal curves generated by the initiator-generator technique. The *quadric Koch curves* have a square as the initiator and have a generator that is made up of line segments that meet at 90-degree angles.

quadric surface. A curved surface which is the locus of all points that satisfy a second-degree polynomial equation having three variables. Depending upon the coefficients of the various terms of the equation, the quadric surface may be a sphere, a paraboloid, an ellipsoid, a cone, a hyperboloid, or a hyperbolic paraboloid.

quadrilateral. Also known as a *quad*. A graphics figure that is defined by four vertices connected by line segments.

quadtree. The organization of two-dimensional space into a tree by starting with a square that encompasses all of the desired space and recursively subdividing squares into four smaller squares until the lowest desired level of detail is reached.

quantization technique. A method for reducing a large number of colors to the limited number available for a particular display mode. Such techniques include *uniform quantization*, use of the *popularity algorithm*, *median cut*, and *octree quantization*.

quantization transform. A 1 to 1 pixel transformation to modify or enhance an image.

quantized noise. A digitally sampled noise signal, which is almost, but not quite, the same as the original analog noise signal.

quantizing. The process of measuring an analog signal to determine its amplitude at sample points determined by a sampling rate chosen for the equipment. The measured amplitude of each sample is then converted to a digital code to produce *pulse code modulation*.

quarter ellipse algorithm. An algorithm that draws a quarter of an ellipse (a curve that spans $\pi/2$ radians of elliptical arc) by performing an affine transformation of a quarter circle.

quartic roots. The roots of a fourth-degree equation. Such an equation can be used to represent a large number of different solids.

quartic surface. A curved surface which is the locus of all points that satisfy a third-degree polynomial equation having three variables. Depending upon the coefficients of the various terms of the equation, various geometric objects may be obtained. One of these is the torus.

quaternion. A set of four numbers, of which one is a scalar and the other three represent the three-dimensional components of a three-dimensional vector having a coordinate system represented by three mutually orthogonal unit vectors i, j, and k. Transformations in three-dimensional space can be implemented with *quaternions* without any singularities occurring.

queue. A number of tasks arranged in a line waiting for processing.

QWERTY keyboard. The standard keyboard, named for the arrangement of the left side of the first row of letters.

R

radial acceleration. Acceleration of a track on a rotating disk toward or away from the center of rotation due to the track not being perfectly centered.

radial sort method. A technique for generating images in which the data base contains *world coordinates* for all surfaces of the model and the computer program determines which surfaces are visible or hidden, depending upon the viewing angle.

radio-frequency interference. (RFI). Electrical noise or unwanted spurious emissions at radio frequencies that interfere with normal transmissions.

radiometer. An instrument used to measure light intensity, or radiance, in actual physical units independent of the human eye's sensitivity to various wavelengths or levels of intensity.

radiosity. An algorithm for rendering graphics scenes through computing the balancing of light energy coming toward and going away from every point on a surface.

RAID. Redundant array of inexpensive or independent disks. A group of disk drives connected by software so that speed of access is increased and so that all data are written twice so that if a single drive fails, no data will be permanently lost.

RAM. Random access memory. Fast access computer memory that can be accessed at any desired location without delay, rather than the computer having to wait for a tape to reach a desired point or a head to be properly positioned on a disk. *RAM* is usually implemented in the form of integrated circuit devices. It is the main source of computer memory.

RAMDAC. Random access memory digital-to-analog converter. A digital-to-analog converter that instead of providing a linear conversion compensates for color or gamma correction through a built-in table contained in RAM.

RAMdisk. A simulated disk consisting of a part of the computer's random access memory. Because the speed of such memory is much faster than that of any type of disk, use of a *RAMdisk* permits computer operations to be done much faster, but since storage is not permanent, at the end of a session, the data must be transferred to a conventional storage device or lost when the computer is turned off.

random access memory. (RAM). Fast access computer memory that can be accessed at any desired location without delay, rather than the computer having to wait for a tape to reach a desired point or a head to be properly positioned on a disk. *RAM* is usually implemented in the form of integrated circuit devices. It is the main source of computer memory.

random access memory digital-to-analog converter. (RAMDAC). A digital-to-analog converter that instead of providing a linear conversion compensates for color or gamma correction through the use of a built-in table contained in RAM.

random fractal. A fractal curve that is generated using a stochastic process.

random iteration algorithm. A technique for rendering pictures of attractors of an iterated function system by starting with a point and randomly performing one of a set of contractive affine transformations.

random noise function. A function that varies randomly between -1 and +1 throughout three-dimensional space with an autocorrelation distance of about 1 in every direction. Also known as the *Perlin noise function*.

random scan. A display in which each vector or character to be displayed on the screen is drawn by direct deflection so that the electron beam is used to trace the actual line or character shape on the screen at the appropriate location. This is in contrast to a *raster scan*, where the beam scans the CRT face in an orderly fashion and is illuminated at those points where a picture element is to be other than black. *Random scan* is faster as long as no complex colored backgrounds are required.

range contrast.   The ratio of the brightest area of a display to the dimmest area.

raster.   The arrangement of pixels as a two-dimensional array or grid in a display monitor.

raster coordinates.   The coordinate system which defines location of pixels on a raster display. By convention, the coordinate (0,0) is at the top left-hand corner of the display.

raster display.   A computer display in which the screen is scanned in an orderly fashion from left to right for each line and then from top to bottom for the frame to produce a rectangular array of pixels. The scanning technique is known as *raster scan* and is the most common method of creating a computer or television display.

raster graphics.   Images that are defined as the colors assigned to a rectangular array of pixels in a column and row format.

raster image processor.   (RIP). The part of a graphics reproducing printer that reads bit-map instructions and translates them into actions of the print mechanism.

raster operation or **raster-op.**   (ROP). Any logical operation such as AND, OR, NOT, NOR, XOR, etc., which is performed on the bit planes of a frame buffer in the course of performing block moves, fades, etc., of video data.

raster rotation.   The rotation of a digitized graphics raster by an arbitrary angle.

raster scan.   A technique used to create a computer or television display, in which the electron beam(s) of a cathode-ray tube are scanned across the face of the tube in an orderly fashion, beginning at the top left corner, traveling from left to right with a slight downward motion, jumping back to the left edge at the next lower line level when the right edge is reached and proceeding thus until the last scan line is drawn, at which point the beam jumps back to the top left corner. At any point on the scanning path the beam(s) may be activated to produce a spot of light of the desired color on the screen.

raster shearing.   The rotation of a raster through the use of shear matrices.

raster space.   The coordinate system that is used to identify the location of pixels when displaying an image on a monitor.

raster text.   Textual characters defined by patterns of pixels that are applied to a monitor image during raster scan.

rasterization.   The process of dividing a picture into pixel-sized elements.

rasterize.   To convert a picture into pixel-sized elements for display on a raster display.

ray rejection test.   In ray tracing, a test that rejects all eye rays that don't intersect with objects in the scene.

ray tracing.   The technique of creating a realistic image by tracing light rays. In *forward ray tracing* all rays of light illuminating a scene are traced from the light source to the object they intersect and then if there are reflections or refractions, the tracing continues until the ray leaves the scene. In *backward ray tracing* rays are traced from the observer to the display screen back to the scene objects and light source. The result is that all reflections and shadows appear in the image without being specifically described in the scene description.

ray-object intersection.   In ray tracing, the intersection of the backward ray that passes from the eye to the screen with some object in the scene. This is the fundamental operation in any ray tracing algorithm.

read-only memory.   (ROM). Memory that stores data permanently. The data can be read as often as desired, but the memory cannot be written to.

real estate distribution.   The assignment of input data to whichever window on a display currently contains the cursor.

real time.   Computer software that can accept incoming data and process and display them as fast as the data occur in the real world.

realistic rendering.   Computer software that attempts to produce images that have all of the lighting, coloring, shadows, reflections, etc., of a real-world scene.

record. (pronounced *REC-ord*). A group of related pieces of data that are treated as a single unit of information.

record. (pronounced *ree-CORD*). To place data on a storage medium.

recording zone. The portion of a disk upon which data can be recorded.

rectilinear domain.   A domain composed of cartesian products of intervals of R.

recto.   In typography, the right-hand page of a book or magazine. The left-hand page is called *verso*.

recursive computation. A mathematical process involving an equation that finds a new value for a variable given that the current value is known. An initial value for the variable is inserted and the equation solved. The new value is then inserted in the equation and the equation solved again to obtain the next value in the series. This process is repeated as often as desired.

red, green, blue. (RGB). The primary colors which are combined at various intensities in an *additive* color system to produce all intermediate shades.

reduced instruction set computing. (RISC). A computer that uses a microprocessor having fewer and faster instructions. Many instructions that are usually built into the microprocessor must be done by software in the RISC microprocessor. However, overall, the RISC is faster than the usual microprocessor system.

redundant array of inexpensive or independent disks. (RAID). A group of disk drives connected by software so that speed of access is increased and so that all data are written twice so that if a single drive fails, no data will be permanently lost.

reentrant polygon clipping. An algorithm used for clipping a polygon to a convex polygonal clipping region. The input polygon is successively clipped to each edge of the clipping region until all edges have been applied. Also known as the *Sutherland-Hodgeman algorithm.*

reference geoid. A standard model for the shape of the earth. The simplest form is a sphere having the mean equatorial radius of the earth.

reference port. The hardware system that serves as a standard for the design and testing of a piece of software.

refinement procedure. A procedure used to create the image of an object in more detail.

reflectance. The ratio of light reflected from the surface of an object to the light incident upon the surface.

reflectance map. An image, often computed as a projection on a cube, used to reduce computation in rendering of reflecting surfaces. It is produced by first computing each point of an image as a function of the direction from the center point of the object and then referencing the image to the directions of reflected rays from the surface of the object. Also known as an *environment map.*

reflection map. An image mapped onto a surface to simulate the mirror-like reflections of other objects in the scene.

reflective read. An optical medium from which data are read by the reflection of a laser beam from the medium.

refraction. The bending of light rays when they pass through the boundary between two dissimilar materials. The *index of refraction* is a measure of this bending and is also equivalent to the ratio of the speed of light in the two mediums.

refresh. 1. To reactivate the phosphor of a cathode-ray screen by repeatedly positioning the electron gun at the same point. This causes the phosphor to glow continually instead of fading after the beam is removed. 2. To recharge cells of a dynamic memory so that data stored in them do not dissipate and get lost.

refresh rate. The rate at which refresh takes place. For U.S. television this is 60 Hz or 60 times per second.

region of interest. (ROI). A portion of an image that is selected for further examination or processing.

registration. The alignment or degree of alignment of two or more images that are to overlay. For example, in color printing, the red, green, yellow, and black ink images must register exactly to produce a quality color picture.

relative address. The address of a datum in computer memory with respect to some reference address already stored in the computer. The sum of the reference address and the *relative address* should be the *absolute address* of the datum. Compare *absolute address*.

relative index of refraction. A measure of the amount of light that is refracted when a light ray passes through the surface of two dissimilar materials.

remote procedure call. (RPC). A software function that is used while a computer is running another program to enable it to run a subprogram on another computer in the same network.

render. To convert a graphics image into an array of pixel colors for display.

RenderMan. Trademark of Pixar, Inc. 1. A proposed standard for interfacing to rendering programs. 2. A high-level program for rendering of realistic graphics scenes developed by Pixar, Inc..

repaint. To replace the current screen image with a new image having the same characteristics. This usually is needed when operations on the screen image have caused some of the original image information to be lost.

repelling periodic orbit. A periodic orbit for which the absolute value of the eigenvalue is greater than one.

residency mask. A bit vector in which each bit is assigned to a cell within partitioned object space. Use to quickly determine which objects in a scene are intersected by a particular ray.

resize. To change the size of a window on a display.

resolution. A measure of the quality of an image. For halftones, this is expressed in lines per inch. For printed material from computer printers, it is usually expressed in dots per inch. For a computer display, resolution is expressed in terms of the number of pixels in the horizontal and vertical directions.

resource. Something that is limited and so must be allocated carefully, such as display screen space, computer memory, or hardware-limited table space.

restitution coefficient. The coefficient that relates velocity of a ball before and after a bounce. It is e in the equation $v_+ = -ev_-$.

retained mode. A graphics processing technique in which rather than rendering each datum as it is input, the datum is stored for later rendering as a group. Contrast with *immediate mode*.

retirement. Discarding of a magnetic tape, magnetic disk, or optical disk when it has too many defects.

retrace. The portion of a video signal during which the scanning electron beam is moved from the end of one scan line to the beginning of the next (*horizontal retrace*) or from the end of one field to the beginning of the next (*vertical retrace*). Video is usually blanked during *retrace* so that retrace lines do not appear on the screen.

retrieval. The recovery of objects from a data base and the display of them upon a screen.

retrieval key. A word or phrase that gives a clue to the contents of a document and is used in searching for documents related to some particular subject.

retroreflectivity. The fraction of light that is returned from a collimated light source for a particular object at a specified angle of incidence and along the line of incidence.

reverse video. Displaying of characters with the opposite of their normal colors (the original background color becomes the color of the character and the original character color becomes the color of the background). Used to highlight a particular line of a display, often one that has been selected by the cursor.

revision bar. A way of indicating parts of a document that have been revised by a line in the margin encompassing the revised text.

rewritable. Media on which data may be erased and rewritten. All magnetic disks are rewritable, but optical disks, with a few exceptions, are not.

RFI. Radio-frequency interference. Electrical noise or unwanted spurious emissions at radio frequencies that interfere with normal transmissions.

RGB. Red, green, blue. The primary colors which are combined at various intensities in an *additive* color system to produce all intermediate shades.

RGB monitor. A color monitor that accepts separate red, green, and blue video signals rather than composite video.

RGB video. Red, green, and blue video signals transmitted separately over individual wires. To drive a monitor, a separate synchronization signal is also required.

rhombic dodecahedron. A twelve-sided solid whose faces are rhombuses.

rhombus. An equilateral parallelogram having its angles oblique.

ribbon. A twisted three-dimensional curve used in modeling molecular structures.

ribbon cable. A flat cable composed of a number of wires arranged in a horizontal plane and held in this position by plastic bonding.

right reading. Normal reproduction of an image from left to right.

ring. A planar object bounded on the outside and inside by concentric circles.

RIP. Raster image processor. The part of a graphics reproducing printer that reads bit-map instructions and translates them into actions of the print mechanism.

RISC. Reduced instruction set computing. A computer that uses a microprocessor having fewer and faster instructions. Many instructions that are usually built into the microprocessor must be done by software in the RISC microprocessor. However, overall, the RISC is faster than the usual microprocessor system.

RLL. Run length limited. A method of data compression in which strings of like bytes are encoded into two bytes, one a number of repetitions and the other the repeated byte value.

robust. Software or algorithm capable of handling unusual cases without failure.

ROI. Region of interest. A portion of an image that is selected for further examination or processing.

rolling-ball algorithm. A technique for mouse-driven three-dimensional orientation control.

ROM. Read-only memory. Memory that stores data permanently. The data can be read as often as desired, but the memory cannot be written to.

root. A node in a hierarchy that has no parent.

ROP. Raster operation. Any logical operation such as AND, OR, NOT, NOR, XOR, etc., which is performed on the bit planes of a frame buffer in the course of performing block moves, fades, etc., of video data.

roping. An aliasing effect in which a line appears to change in color, brightness, or width to produce a pattern suggestive of a braided rope.

rotation. The turning of an object around a specified axis.

rotation matrix. A matrix that is used to multiply a vector to cause a rotation of the vector.

Roth diagram. A diagram used in ray-tracing models in which constructive solid geometry is used to represent the path of a ray including regions inside and outside the composite model.

Rothstein code. A binary sequence that describes a line whose slope is q/p.

roughness. The property of the surface of an object that causes scattering of the light that reflects from it. A smooth surface causes little scattering and appears like a mirror; a rough surface causes a great deal of scattering.

round off. To end a number after a certain number of digits with the last digit increased by one if the next (unused) digit is greater than or equal to 5 and the last digit left the same otherwise.

router. A CADD software system that converts a wire list into a printed circuit board layout, routing each of the wires to minimize crossovers.

RPC. Remote procedure call. A software function that is used while a computer is running another program to enable it to run a subprogram on another computer in the same network.

RS-170A. An IEEE standard for composite video that is the same as the NTSC composite video.

RS-232. An IEEE standard for serial interfaces such as those between computers and printers, terminals, modems, mice, etc. Now superseded by RS-488.

rubber-banding. A technique for scaling the size of an object in a computer drawing by selecting a reference point on the object and then using the cursor to move another point away from or closer to the first point selected. All of the other points on the object except the selected point move so as to preserve the shape of the object.

rubber-stamping. Replicating a two-dimensional object on a graphics display by selecting a point on it with the cursor and then dragging that point to a new location where another copy of the object is placed.

run-length limited. (RLL). A method of data compression in which strings of like bytes are encoded into two bytes, one a number of repetitions and the other the repeated byte value.

runarounds. In typography, lines of irregular length that are used to surround an irregularly shaped figure.

S

sample point. In antialiasing, a sample point is one of several locations within a pixel for which color or z-distance is computed. The results obtained for all sample points are averaged in some way to determine the pixel color.

sampling. The process of converting an analog representation (such as a continuously variable voltage or a mathematical equation) into discrete (usually digital) values by measuring the value at the corresponding discrete points in time.

sampling theorem. A theorem that states that a continuous signal can be reconstructed perfectly from its samples if it is appropriately bandlimited before sampling.

San Marco dragon. A fractal Julia set whose constant term is the real number 3. So-named because it somewhat resembles the skyline of the Basilica in Venice together with its reflection in a flooded square.

sans serif. In typography, those typefaces which do not have filleted decorations at the edges and ends of the letters and which usually do not have variations in stroke width. Examples are Gothic and Helvetica typefaces. Compare with *serif*.
This is a sans serif typeface.
This is a serif typeface.

Sanson-Flamsteed sinusoidal projection. A mapping of a sphere onto a plane that uses the central meridian as the axis of constant spacing. This technique can produce a map that preserves area.

Sarkovskii's theorem. A powerful theorem used in determining the periodicity of points in one-dimensional dynamical systems. The theorem states that if we order all real numbers as follows:

$$3 \vartriangleright 5 \vartriangleright 7 \vartriangleright \ldots \vartriangleright 2 \times 3 \vartriangleright 2 \times 5 \vartriangleright 2 \times 7 \vartriangleright \ldots \vartriangleright 2^2 \times 3 \vartriangleright 2^2 \times 5 \vartriangleright 2^2 \times 7 \vartriangleright \ldots$$
$$\vartriangleright 2^3 \times 3 \vartriangleright 2^3 \times 5 \vartriangleright 2^3 \times 7 \vartriangleright \ldots \vartriangleright 2^4 \vartriangleright 2^3 \vartriangleright 2^2 \vartriangleright 2 \vartriangleright 1$$

then if F has a periodic point of period n and $n \vartriangleright k$, then F also has a periodic point of period k.

saturated recording. A technique for optical recording in which the medium stops absorbing light when a one is fully written, thereby permitting consistent recording despite laser beam variations in intensity and/or focus.

saturation. The amount that a color is composed of the pure color. High saturation colors consist of the color frequency band to a high degree. Low saturation colors contain a great deal of white and thereby appear as pastels.

scalar. Represented by a single number or dimension. Compare *vector* which is a representation by a set of numbers that describe a multi-dimensional space.

scale. The ratio of the size of units in a drawing or model to the size of the units in the actual object that is being pictured.

scaling. Changing the size of characters or graphics.

scallop shell. A fractal Julia set having as its constant term the real number 1.

scan. To convert pictures or printed pages of text into computer-readable code such as ASCII characters or bit maps.

scan conversion. The process of converting an image into scan lines that can be displayed on a raster scan monitor.

scan converter. A device that converts one video format (consisting of a particular horizontal and vertical resolution) to another. In addition to modifying the video to fit the new scanned structure, synchronization signals must be provided.

scan head. The part of a scanner that optically senses text or graphics as it moves across a page.

scan rate. The rate at which a scanner samples an image in samples per second.

scanline. 1. A horizontal line of a raster display. In synchronism with the scanning of the display beam, the video for the scan line must vary to represent the colors of each of the pixels in the line. 2. A row of pixels.

scanline algorithm. A technique for rendering an image in which the image is rendered one scanline at a time, rather than on an object-by-object basis.

scanner. A device which moves across a page, optically sensing text or graphics and, with the aid of software, converts what is read to computer-readable code.

scattering. The dispersal of light in many directions when it is reflected from a point on a surface.

scene description. The specifying of a scene in terms of objects, light sources, and viewing devices as an initial step in rendering the scene.

schematic capture. The use of a CAD system to construct a schematic diagram using a set of symbols included in the software and allowing the user to select symbols and interconnect them with lines representing wires.

Schumacher algorithm. An algorithm for creating a priority list of clusters of convex polygons, using a plane tree structure.

scientific visualization. The creation of computer graphics images that show the relationships among incoming data.

scissoring. A technique for clipping an image at the boundaries of a screen, using hardware tailored for the purpose.

scoptic. Achromatic vision in dim light using the rods in the eye. Compare to *photopic*.

screen. 1. The display surface of a cathode-ray tube or other display device. 2. A grid of fine wires through which an image is photographed to break it into dots and produce a halftone.

screen angles. Angles at which halftone screens are oriented with respect to the image to avoid moire patterns. In creating four-color separation negatives, the commonly used angles are 45 degrees for black, 75 degrees for magenta, 90 degrees for yellow, and 105 degrees for cyan.

screen capture. To transfer the contents of a display screen to a computer file.

screen coordinates. The coordinate system used to define the position of a pixel on the display screen.

screen door transparency. A graphics technique in which surfaces are rendered by only a pattern instead of solid color, so that occluded objects are partially visible.

screen dump. To transfer the contents of a display screen to a printer.

screen extent. The size of the rectangle enclosing an image to be displayed.

screen font. Data designed to display a type font on the display screen that is a close match in size and style for a similar font that is to be used by the printer. This gives a display that looks very much like the final printed product.

screen size. The diagonal of the rectangle within which an image may be displayed on a screen. This measure became common when round display tubes were used, when it corresponded to the useful diameter of the CRT.

scroll bars. Rectangular regions bordering a window which, when accessed by the cursor, control the scrolling of the window contents.

scroll rate. The rate at which an image moves in a fixed window when scrolling.

scrolling. The moving of an entire image up or down on the display screen so that new material appears at the top or bottom of the screen and old material is dropped off at the bottom or top.

SCSI.   Small computer system interface. An industry standard for interfacing peripheral devices to a personal computer. It includes definitions for both hardware and software.

sculptured surface.   A free-form surface, i.e., one that cannot be represented by a simple mathematical equation.

SECAM.   Systeme Électronique Couleur Avec Memoire. The color television standard used by France and the former Soviet nations. Because of the lack of equipment designed for this particular system, pictures are usually recorded and stored using the PAL system and encoded in the SECAM format just prior to transmission.

section plane.   A plane used to mark the position at which an object is cut to provide a cut-away view.

section space.   A clipping volume that is defined by a collection of planes defined in world coordinates.

sector.   The smallest addressable unit on a magnetic or optical disk. Usually contains 512 bytes.

seed fill.   A technique for filling a connected two-dimensional region with a color or pattern in which a point is selected within the polygon, and the color or pattern is extended in all directions until the polygon boundaries are encountered. Algorithms for *seed filling* need to be carefully designed to make sure that all parts of peculiarly shaped polygons are filled. Also known as *flood fill*.

seek error.   An error in reading a disk in which the disk system is unable to locate one of the sectors that comprise the file addressed by the user.

segment.   1. A curve or straight line that makes up part of a more complex curve. 2. In the GKS standard, a set of attributes and primitives. 3. A section of memory that may be switched in or out of working memory by a memory manager.

selective erase.   The erasing of certain objects in a graphics image without affecting the other objects.

selector. An electronic device that switches between inputs or outputs as dictated by a control signal.

self-affine. A function that has more than one scaling factor.

self-intersection. The property of a curve or surface where it intersects itself.

self-similarity. A property of a geometric figure in which the overall shape of the figure is duplicated at smaller and smaller scales as the figure is enlarged. See also *fractal*.

sensitivity. A measure of the amplitude of a signal needed to record data on a magnetic or optical disk or an image on a film.

separating plane tree. A data structure consisting of objects separated by mathematical planes in such a way as to facilitate placing the objects in occlusion order of priority.

separation plane method. A technique for rendering images that makes use of an imaginary plane between objects. This can be used with the results of a hidden surface algorithm to determine which object is nearest the viewpoint and permits drawing of the farthest object first.

serial. A data communications method in which each data bit is transmitted sequentially.

serialization. Processing of data sent serially from a source in the same order that it was received.

serif. A class of typefaces having small filleted decorations at the ends of strokes and horizontal strokes that are thinner than vertical strokes. Compare with *sans serif*.
This is a serif typeface.
This is a sans serif typeface.

serpentine raster pattern. A raster scan in which odd scanlines are traversed left-to-right and even lines traversed right-to-left.

server. The computer in a network which controls all requests from other computers for data access.

shader. A graphics subroutine that computes the effects of illumination upon a visible surface and thereby determines the pixel colors.

shading. The assignment of shades of color to the surfaces of a graphics object to represent the visual effects of light sources upon the object. See *Gourad shading* and *Phong shading*.

shading model. The algorithm or equation that computes the effects of light upon a surface and determines the shade of color to be used for a particular point or surface. Also known as an *illumination model* or *lighting model*.

shadow algorithm. An algorithm or equation used to determine if a point or surface is in the shadow of an object and if so, what its color should be.

shadow depth map. A technique for determining the shadows in a scene by performing z-buffer scanconversion and visibility determination of the scene from the perspective of a light source and then storing only the depth information in a 2-D array.

shadow map. An array having a member for each direction that a ray travels from the viewpoint in rendering a scene, with each member containing the distance to the first object encountered by the ray. Used to test if object surfaces are illuminated or in shadow.

shadow mask. A perforated metal plate that is positioned between the electron gun and the phosphor of a cathode-ray tube in such a manner that the beam from each electron gun passes through the proper hole to activate a phosphor dot of the corresponding color.

shadow theorem. The random shift dynamical system orbit on the overlapping attractor A is the shadow of a deterministic orbit on $\breve{A}$.

shaft culling. A method of computing a list of potential occluders for a given source-receiver pair. The source is totally visible when the list is empty. If an object in the list cuts the shaft, the source is totally occluded. In other cases, shadow rays are traced to determine the shadow characteristics.

sharpening. An image processing technique that enhances edges and fine details of the image.

sharpening filter. A filter used to enhance the differences between the pixels that make up an image, thereby causing an edge-sharpening effect.

shear. A coordinate transformation which involves changing the angles between axes.

shear matrix. A 2×2 matrix having a diagonal of all 1's and a determinant of 1. Used in raster rotation.

shuffle generator. A table of numbers used to jitter a function so that any spatial patterns resulting from sampling are removed.

siccade. The long-range action of the eye as it repositions from one object to another. Visual input is suppressed during siccade and for a short time afterward.

Siegel disk. A fractal curve that is a complement of a Julia set using the iterated equation $z_{n+1} = az_n + z^2$.

Sierpinski triangle. A fractal curve that can be created by starting with a filled-in equilateral triangle and removing the triangle created by connecting the midpoints of the sides. This leaves four filled-in equilateral triangles for which the same process is repeated, and the procedure then continues for as long as desired. The curve is

Sierpinski Triangle

interesting because it turns out that if the proper parameters are inserted in a lot of different fractal generating methods, the result is a Sierpinski triangle. Also known as an *arrowhead*.

Sierra error diffusion filter. An algorithm for performing discrete convolution or digital filtering, which is the improving of the appearance of an image by replacing a pixel by some function of that pixel and its neighbors. It is frequently used to change color images to images consisting of black, white, and shades of gray.

SIGGRAPH. 1. The Special Interest Group for Graphics of the Association for Computer Machinery. It is one of the major organizations for computer graphics professionals. 2. An annual conference for computer professionals held in late July or early August, sponsored by SIGGRAPH.

signal-to-noise ratio. (SNR). The ratio of signal power to unwanted noise power in an analog electronic signal. This is usually expressed in *decibels*, which are 10 times the logarithm of the ratio.

signature analysis. The comparison of a function computed from the outputs of a digital circuit with a prestored value to determine whether the circuit is functioning properly.

silhouette edge. An edge obtained by tracing the outer boundary of the two-dimensional representation of a graphics object. It separates all of the pixels dedicated to the object from the rest of an image.

Silicon Valley. A portion of the Santa Clara Valley of California starting approximately 50 miles south of San Francisco, so called because of the large number of companies in the area that specialize in the design and development of transistors and integrated circuits composed of silicon.

silver. A common precious metal, many of whose salts are light sensitive. These salts are used as the light-sensitive emulsion for photographic film and printing paper.

simplices. A set of primitive shapes that includes triangles, tetrahedra, etc.

simploids. A set of shapes that includes both simplices and boxes (such as square, cube, etc.).

simulation. The representation of a real life situation, a mathematical algorithm, or an electronic circuit by a software model so that the *simulation* can be run with various parameters to determine how the real case will behave.

sinc function. The function $\dfrac{\sin x}{x}$.

sine fractal. A fractal curve produced by iterating the equation

$$z_n = \sin(z_{n-1}) + c$$

with $z_0 = 0 + i0$ and c varied over the complex plane.

sink. 1. A heavy piece of metal, often finned, that is used to draw heat away from a heat-producing electronic component. 2. In typography, extra white space at the top of a published page that is used to emphasize the body text.

sinusoid. A curve produced by plotting the sine or cosine function.

skew. To slant a selected character or graphics object.

skew transform. A geometric transformation that changes the angle between the coordinate axes, resulting in a change in the shape of all figures being transformed.

skitter. A coordinate system placed on the surface of an object to define possible directions of movement.

slerp. Spherical linear interpolation. A method of interpolating between two quaternions by following the shortest path between them on a sphere.

slew rate. 1. The rate of change of the output of a servo system as it changes to lock in on a new input signal. 2. The rate at which a display system pans through an image file.

slice. To apply section-plane clipping to an object space.

Smale's horseshoe map. A physical system characterized by having a strange attractor.

small computer system interface. (SCSI). An industry standard for interfacing peripheral devices to a personal computer. It includes definitions for both hardware and software.

SMD. Surface mount device. An electronic component that is designed to mount on the surface of a printed circuit board without drilling any mounting holes. It is usually attached by wave soldering.

smearing. Modifying the color of a pixel with some function of adjacent pixel colors to smooth out violent discontinuities in a picture.

smooth shading. The shading of a graphics surface by continuously varying the color tones over the surface in accordance with the way the surface is illuminated. This is the most difficult shading technique. *Phong* *shading* and *Gouraud shading* are simplified techniques for accomplishing an approximation of *smooth shading* while reducing the computer computations required.

smoothing. The reduction of noise effects in an image by spreading of the noise over a larger area.

SMPTE. Society of Motion Picture and Television Engineers. The professional organization for engineers working in motion pictures or television.

SMT. Surface mount technology. The technology by which *SMD*s are soldered to printed circuit boards.

snap. In a CAD system, a process whereby the cursor is automatically moved to the nearest point on an existing line or grid.

Snell's law. The law that expresses the relationship that governs the refraction of light. The law states that the sine of the incident angle of light to a surface of an object is equal to the refractive index of the material multiplied by the sine of the refracted angle.

snow. The image produced by the display of noise on a video screen.

snowflake halls. A self-similar fractal curve created using the initiator-generator technique. It uses an eleven segment generator having two different length line segments.

snowflake, Koch. A self-similar fractal curve created using the initiator-generator technique. It has an appearance similar to a snowflake.

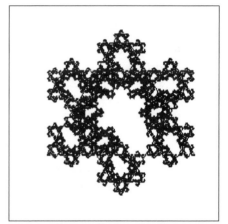

Snowflake Halls

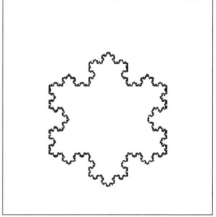

Koch Snowflake

SNR. Signal-to-noise ratio. The ratio of signal power to unwanted noise power in an analog electronic signal. This is usually expressed in *decibels*, which are 10 times the logarithm of the ratio.

snub figure. A solid formed by surrounding the edges of each of a regular solid's faces with equilateral triangles.

Sobel operators. A pair of 3×3 matrices used to sharpen the edges of objects in an image.

Society of Motion Picture and Television Engineers. (SMPTE). The professional organization for engineers working in motion pictures or television.

Soddy's formula. A formula for the radius of a circle inscribed in the curvilinear triangle formed by three tangent circles. The formula is

$$\frac{1}{r} = \frac{1}{a} + \frac{1}{b} + \frac{1}{c} + 2\sqrt{\frac{1}{bc} + \frac{1}{ac} + \frac{1}{ab}}$$

where a, b, and c are the radii of the tangent circles and r is the radius of the inscribed circle.

soft copy. A copy of digital data on a storage medium that cannot be read with the human eye, such as a floppy or hard disk, an optical disk, or a magnetic tape. Compare with *hard copy*.

soft return. A carriage return character inserted into text by a word processor to mark the end of a line and cause the processor to wrap around to the beginning of the next line to print or display the next word. The *soft return* is automatically repositioned as required when text changes are made.

solid modeling. The rendering of a scene described in terms of graphics primitives by converting to two dimensions and directly computing surface colors. Uses constructive solid geometry techniques.

solid texture. A texture pattern that is defined in three-dimensional space so that volumes cut out of the object will reveal the proper internal texture pattern.

sonic tablet. A digitizing table composed of a surface having strip microphones along a horizontal and vertical edge. A stylus is used to mark the desired position. Ultrasound pulses from the stylus are picked up by the microphones and the time delay of the signals used to determine the selected position.

spaghetti model. Storage of spatial data in the form of a list of *(x,y)* coordinates without any other information.

span. A set of pixels that comprise the portion of a scanline between edges of a convex polygon.

spatial. Pertaining to three-dimensional space.

SPEC Benchmark Suite. System Performance Evaluation Cooperative Benchmark Suite. A set of software routines designed to test the speed of various aspects of computer performance. A quasi-standard agreed to by a group of companies that are leaders in computer system design.

special effect. In flight simulation graphics, a visual effect produced using animated images to represent, for example, a fire burning.

speckle. A nonadditive noise effect resulting when local interference patterns are produced by monochromatic (laser) light reflecting from surfaces whose roughness is of the same order as the light wavelength.

spectrophotometer. An instrument used to measure the light intensity for a selected narrow frequency band.

specular reflection. The reflection of light from a mirrorlike or very shiny object.

sphere. The locus in three dimensions of all points equidistant from a given center point.

spherical linear interpolation. A method of interpolating between two quaternions by following the shortest path between them on a sphere. Also known as *slerp*.

spherical product surface. The surface generated using two curves whose *x* and *y* components are defined by parametric equations. Each point on the surface is defined by taking the product of the *x* coordinates of the two curves as the x coordinate and the product of the y coordinates of the two curves as the y coordinate. A sphere is obtained if the two curves are circles.

spin-up. The time from applying power to a disk drive until the disk has accelerated to the normal operating speed.

spindle. The center part of a disk drive which is located at the axis of rotation and which provides the force that causes the disk to rotate.

spline. A mathematically defined curve that provides a smooth path from one point to another with a shape controlled by a number of control points. See *B-spline*.

spraying. A feature of a software painting program that simulates the action of a spray gun.

sprite. A small moveable graphics pattern on a display, often used in video game animation.

staircasing. The representation of a straight line in a graphics image as a jagged staircase-like pattern, as a result of aliasing effects.

stencil. A method of storing color data in frame buffers in which the ones in an incoming bit pattern cause the corresponding pixels in the frame buffer to be overwritten and the zeroes cause the corresponding pixels to be left alone.

stereo. A truly three-dimensional picture produced by creating two separate images, one for each of the two human eyes and viewed from its viewpoint. On cathode-ray tubes, the images may be side by side, viewed through an optical combining device; or an image in red may be superimposed on an image in blue and the result viewed through glasses, one having a red lens and the other a blue lens. Other techniques make use of different polarizations for the two images.

stereographic map. A mapping of a sphere onto a plane where the point of projection is at the tangent point's opposite pole. It is both conformal and circle preserving.

Stevenson-Arce error diffusion filter. An algorithm for performing discrete convolution or digital filtering, which is the improving of the appearance of an image by replacing a pixel by some function of that pixel and its neighbors. It is frequently used to change color images to images consisting of black, white, and shades of gray.

stilb. A unit of luminance equal to 1/1000th nit.

stipple. 1. A pattern of dots or short dashes. 2. A pattern of dots used to fill a background.

stochastic sampling. An antialiasing technique that computes a sequence of images. For each pixel, a different sample point is used in each of the images. The final pixel color is the average for that pixel in each of the images. In computation, only a single frame need be stored, containing the average value for each pixel up to that point in the computation. Each new set of values is averaged into the value contained in the frame.

storage media. The physical material upon which data are recorded such as magnetic disks, optical disks, or magnetic tape.

strange attractor. A set of values on which many orbits of a dynamical set of equations tend to land.

streaking. An error in displaying or computing an image that causes objects to extend horizontally beyond their actual boundaries.

stretching. Changing the shape of graphics objects by changing the scale in one axis direction and decreasing it in the orthogonal axis direction.

string. A series of characters.

strip. A mesh of triangles or quads which is only one triangle or quad wide.

stroke. A short straight line segment used as part of a vector graphics image.

stroke device. An input device, such as a mouse or digitizing tablet, that provides a sequence of sets of point coordinates.

stroke display or **stroker.** A type of cathode-ray tube display in which lines and characters are drawn by directly moving the electron beam to trace out the desired shape rather than scanning the beam in a raster and illuminating the appropriate points in the raster scan. Also known as a *calligraphic display*.

stroke text. Text characters that are defined in terms of lines, making it easy to scale text size.

strong. A color that is relatively high in color saturation and color value.

structure text. Text that is to be scaled, rotated, put into perspective, etc.

Stucki error diffusion filter. An algorithm for performing discrete convolution or digital filtering, which is the improving of the appearance of an image by replacing a pixel by some function of that pixel and its neighbors. It is frequently used to change color images to images consisting of black, white, and shades of gray.

style. 1. In line drawing, the type of line, whether solid, dotted, dashed, center line, etc. 2. In typography, a variation of a basic typeface, such as italic, bold, etc.

stylus. A pen-like instrument used with a graphics tablet to obtain position information for input to a computer.

subatomic primitive. A graphics primitive that is at a level below a primitive object, such as the definition of a portion of a scanline.

subdivision. Recursively dividing a line, curve, or surface into smaller and smaller segments.

subpixel. A subdivision of a pixel used to render one part of the pixel separately so that the results from several *subdivisions* can be combined in some weighted fashion to obtain an antialiased value for the pixel.

subscript. A character that is reduced in size and printed below the baseline for a line of text characters.

subtractive color model. The color model used for mixing paints and inks, where the pigments absorb some colors and reflect others. The basic colors are cyan, magenta, and yellow. In addition black is often used to produce a richer picture. When two or more layers of different colored ink are superimposed, the apparent color is the reflected color, which is what remains after each layer of ink has absorbed its characteristic part of the light spectrum.

succolarity. The property in a fractal curve of having filaments that nearly fill space. Term coined by Benoit Mandelbrot in 1977.

superattractive periodic orbit. A periodic orbit for which the absolute value of the eigenvalue is equal to zero.

superblack. A level below that of black in a composite video signal. It is used for synchronizing color information.

supercase. In typography, a set of characters that are neither upper nor lowercase. On a keyboard, they are accessed by first hitting a key designated for a *supershift* code.

superconic. An extension of the conic curve in which the terms of the conic equation are raised to an arbitrary power to vary the shape and smoothness of the curve.

superimpose. To place a partially transparent image over another image so that portions of both images appear in the final composite image.

superquadric. An extension of quadric surfaces formed by computing the *spherical product surface* of two *superconics*.

superred, supergreen, superblue. The primary colors of the CIE color space. They are not physically realizable because they would require negative intensities, but are useful in specifying the components of realizable colors.

supersampling. The rendering of several sample points within a single pixel so that the resulting values can be combined in some weighted fashion to produce antialiasing.

superscript. A character that is reduced in size and printed above the baseline for a line of text characters.

supershift. In typography, a key on the keyboard that produces a code that allows access to *supercase* characters.

supertwist. A liquid crystal display (LCD) device in which the crystals are twisted to provide a wider viewing angle and greater contrast than an ordinary LCD.

Super-VGA. A display graphics interface card that complies fully with the characteristics of the IBM Video Graphics Array (VGA) and also offers a number of advanced video modes not supported by IBM.

superwhite. A high-intensity white that is 10 percent higher in voltage than white signals obtained from normal images. It can be used to display a cursor that does not disappear when it is moved to the white area of a display.

surface mapping. Projecting a two-dimensional image or pattern from the plane on which it was defined onto a curved or flat surface.

surface modeling. A technique for representing solid objects on a two-dimensional display.

surface mount device. (SMD). An electronic component that is designed to mount on the surface of a printed circuit board without drilling any mounting holes. It is usually attached by wave soldering.

surface mount technology. (SMT). The technology by which SMDs are soldered to printed circuit boards.

surface normal. A unit vector at a specified point on a graphics surface that is perpendicular to a plane which is tangent to the surface at that point.

surface of revolution. A three-dimensional solid that is defined as the locus of all points on a curve that is swept around a central axis.

Sutherland-Hodgeman algorithm. An algorithm used for clipping a polygon to a convex polygonal clipping region. The input polygon is successively clipped to each edge of the clipping region until all edges have been applied. Also known as *reentrant polygon clipping.*

swash character. In typography, an alternate to a standard alphabetic character that has a curved flourish that extends over or under adjacent characters.

sweeping. 1. Generating a three-dimensional surface by sweeping a two-dimensional curve over a trajectory. 2. The scanning of a cathode-ray tube face by the electron beam to produce a raster scan.

swept contour. A three-dimensional shape produced by translating a contour along a straight line or by rotating it about an axis.

swimming. An instability of a video image that makes portions of the image move in an undulating pattern. This is particularly likely to occur in interlaced scanned images.

swizzle. To reverse the order of bits in a byte from left-to-right to right-to-left.

symbolic link. A tag that dictates how data are to be routed indirectly to a file in a computer file system rather than having the data sent directly.

synchronous. A data stream that is timed by a master clock.

System Performance Evaluation Cooperative (SPEC) **Benchmark Suite.** A set of software routines designed to test the speed of various aspects of computer performance. A quasi-standard agreed to by a group of companies that are leaders in computer system design.

swabbing. Converting an image file from one format to another.

T

tablet. An input device used with a stylus or puck to input the position of the stylus or puck on the tablet to the computer.

tagged image file format. (TIFF). A very flexible format for storing monochrome or color graphics images in the form of bit maps.

Takagi fractal curve. A fractal curve constructed by positive midpoint displacements.

tape backup. A magnetic tape copy of all files on a hard disk.

tape drive. A device that transports magnetic tape past a head that reads or writes data.

Tchebychev fractal curve. A fractal produced by iterating one of the Tchebychev family of orthogonal polynomials over the complex plane.

TCP/IP. Transmission control protocol/internet program. A set of protocols developed for the U.S. Defense Department and used to link computers of dissimilar architectures across networks.

teleconferencing. Conducting a conference among two or more parties at different locations by means of closed-circuit television. The video is often compressed to fit the bandwidth limitations of telephone circuits.

teletex. Encoded text hidden in a broadcast video signal for decoding and display on specially equipped television receivers. Particularly used for transmission of closed-caption information for deaf viewers.

television. An electronics signal that consists of horizontal and vertical synchronization signals and video levels for successive frames of a moving picture. At the receiving end, the synchronization signals are used to synchronize the raster sweep of a cathode-ray tube and the video is displayed as pictures on the CRT screen.

template matching. Detection of an image feature in image processing by convoluting the image with a template consisting of an array containing the feature searched for and thresholding the output.

temporal. Varying with time, such as the change in frame images for frames of an animation sequence as time varies.

temporal aliasing. An undesirable strobing effect in an animation sequence resulting from abrupt changes in the scene from one frame to the next.

tension. The relative amount of curvature near the control points of a curve or surface whose shape is controlled by control points such as a Bezier or B-spline curve.

tensor product. A mathematical matrix function used to generate a curved surface from two orthogonal sets of splines.

tent filter. A filter whose frequency response is in the shape of a triangle.

terabyte. 1024 gigabytes, or 1,099,511,627,776 bytes of data.

teraflop. One trillion (10^{12}) floating point computer operations per second.

terminate and stay resident. (TSR). A method of exiting a software program so that the program remains in computer memory ready to be accessed instantly whenever desired.

tessellate. To subdivide a surface into a number of simpler figures. For example, a polygon can be divided into a number of triangles.

test suite. A set of inputs that is applied to a software system in testing together with the results expected from these inputs.

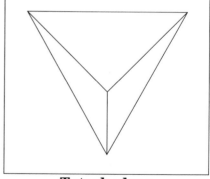

Tetrahedron

tetrahedron. A regular solid having four faces.

T$_E$X. A trademark of the American Mathematical Society for a comprehensive typesetting software system that contains extensive capabilities for the writing of mathematical equations.

texel. A set of data that describes a three-dimensional texture pattern including surface and lighting model data.

text based. The storage of data in the form of character codes rather than graphics techniques.

text file. A data file that consists entirely of character codes such as *ASCII* or *EBCDIC*.

text mode. A display mode in which only a set of predetermined characters can be displayed as contrasted to graphics mode, in which each pixel can be accessed and colored separately.

textual. Consisting entirely of text, with no graphics data.

texture. The properties of a surface that result in changes in the color at different points on the surface. For example, wood grain or marble textures.

texture map. An image that is mapped to a surface to specify its texture. Also known as a *decal*.

TGA. A file format for 24-bit color images in uncompressed form. Originally developed for Truevision's TARGA video adapter boards.

thermal dye transfer printing. A system of high-quality color printing in which dyes are selectively transferred from a plastic medium to paper.

3-D graphics. A graphics system in which a three-dimensional data set is converted to two dimensions for viewing.

threshold. A predetermined level of signal amplitude above which the signal is considered to represent a one and below which it represents a zero.

threshold dithering. A method of digitizing an image using a dithering matrix to vary the threshold between black and white, thereby reducing the amount of aliasing.

thumbwheel. A positioning device that consists of a wheel-like knob partially exposed through a slot in a panel where it can be rotated by the thumb.

tick marks. Small orthogonal lines drawn at intervals across the axes of a graph to indicate distance.

TIFF. Tagged image file format. A very flexible format for storing monochrome or color graphics images in the form of bit maps.

tiling. Constructing a large graphics image by repeating over and over a small graphics image until the available display space is filled.

Timmer's method. A method of implicit curve approximation where intersections of the implicit curve with a predetermined grid are first determined, and then the curve inside each grid cell is traced to determine how to connect the intersections.

token. A bit pattern that is used for identification of a specific action rather than as a binary number.

toner. A dry powder ink that can be electrically charged. In laser printers, etc., the toner is attracted to an electrically charged drum, transferred by contact from the drum to a sheet of paper, and then fixed to the paper permanently by the application of heat.

toolkit. A set of utility programs, usually furnished along with a main program to perform special infrequently used applications not included in the main program.

top-down model. A model that is designed by first modeling the overall structure and then filling in the details.

topological model. A model of three-dimensional data, particularly of geographical surfaces, containing all of the information necessary to examine relationships between various surfaces.

topology. The set of geometric properties related to connectivity, particularly the definition of nodes and their interconnection and constraints on pathways around interconnected networks.

torus. A doughnut-shaped three-dimensional object. It is the locus of all points on a circle swept around a larger orthogonal circle.

torus, Fichter-Hunt. The surface swept out by two series-connected rotational linkages.

touch screen. A display screen designed so that a desired position on the screen may be selected and the cursor moved to that position simply by touching the screen at that point.

track. 1. The path on magnetic or optical media that is followed by the head in recording or reading data. 2. The track followed by the head for one complete revolution of the recording media.

track ball. A caged ball whose upper surface is rotated to position a cursor on a display screen. It is essentially a mouse turned upside down.

tracking. 1. The automatic following of a moving target. 2. In typography, the control of the spacing between letters and words to achieve a desired density of text.

tracking servo. A feedback mechanism that senses variations in track position in recording media, caused by minor defects, and makes corrections in the head position so it is kept centered on the track.

transformation. A function that is applied to the points of a coordinate system to redefine their position. This can be used to change to a different coordinate system or to change the size, shape, or position of an object by rotation, scaling, or translation.

transformation matrix. A 4×4 matrix used to specify a transformation.

translation. The changing of the position of an object through a combination of linear motions each parallel to one of the coordinate axes.

translucent. Partially transparent. The color of an image viewed through a translucent material is usually less pure and the shapes are often blurred.

transmission coefficient. The fraction of the intensity of light remaining after traveling a unit distance through a volume.

transmission control protocol/internet program. (TCP/IP). A set of protocols developed for the U.S. Defense Department and used to link computers of dissimilar architectures across networks.

transparency. The quality of an object of being able to see through it to view objects that are behind it.

transparent. 1. Capable of being seen through. 2. Software or hardware that is automatically invoked and performs its function without the user being aware that it is there.

traversal. The process of sequentially addressing and processing the elements of a display list.

traversal coherence. The coherence of pixels when an image is scanned.

tree-structured directories. A familiar name for a hierarchical file system. The file management system used in DOS which allows a disk to have directories that are divided up into subdirectories that are divided into subsubdirectories, etc.

triangulate. 1. To locate a distant point by taking two separated bearings and computing the triangle geometry. 2. To divide a polygon into triangles to simplify rendering.

triboluminescence. Light generated when certain minerals are rubbed together such as rubbing one quartz crystal against another or rubbing corundum (aluminum oxide) against a metal.

trichromic. The representation of colors as levels of the red, green, and blue (RGB) primary colors.

trigger. A pulse used to initiate an event.

trim curve. A curve that is used to mark the boundary of a surface.

trim marks. Marks on an uncut document that show where it is to be cut to be of the proper size to fit into a final document.

Trinitron. A trademark of Sony Corp. for a type of color cathode-ray tube that uses in-line electron guns to illuminate phosphors that are laid down on the screen surface in stripes rather than as clumps of dots as occurs in conventional color CRT design.

tristimulus values. The *X, Y,* and *Z* coordinates of a color value in the CIE color space.

truncate. To end a number after a certain number of digits, ignoring any digits that may come afterward. (A number may be truncated with no problem at any point after the decimal point. If truncated to the left of the decimal point, the fact that the last digit shown is not a units digit must be indicated in some way.)

TSR. Terminate and stay resident. A method of exiting a software program so that the program remains in computer memory ready to be accessed instantly whenever desired.

tweening. Short for *inbetweening.* 1. (v.) The computation of graphics objects that form intermediate steps between an initial image and a final image. Used especially in animation when the beginning and end frames of a sequence are known but additional frames must be inserted between these to produce the apparent action. 2. (n.) A frame produced by inbetweening.

Twin Dragon Fractal

twin dragon. A fractal curve drawn using the L-systems or initiator-generator technique which has the appearance of a dragon. It is a variation of the *Harter-Heightway dragon curve* in which the dragon is drawn a second time in the reverse direction on the initial starting line. The two curves fit together perfectly.

twisted pair. A type of cable consisting of two wires twisted together to reduce noise pickup and having no shielding. Used for telephone lines and for interconnecting computer networks.

two-and-a-half dimensions.   A two-dimensional graphic in which a three-dimensional effect is produced by assigning an occlusion priority to overlapping objects.

2-D graphics.   A graphics image in which all objects are two dimensional and coplanar.

type font.   A set of characters, letters, and digits of the same type style and size. When moveable type was common, a font consisted of a certain number of pieces of type for each character, the number depending upon the frequency with which each character was used. (For example, a font contained a lot more *e*'s than *z*'s. With electronic type fonts a font refers to only a single occurrence of each character.

type style.   1. In line drawing, the type of line, whether solid, dotted, dashed, center line, etc. 2. In typography, a variation of a basic typeface, such as italic, bold, etc.

U

ultrafiche. A form of microfiche that can hold 1000 document pages per sheet, as contrasted to normal microfiche, which holds 270 pages per sheet.

unbundled. Hardware or software sold separately from each other, rather than sold together as a complete package.

underscan. The scanning of a display screen so that the scan does not cover the entire screen face, leaving a border around the edges.

unerase. To recover a file that has been accidently erased. This is possible in MS-DOS because an *erase* command does not actually remove the contents of the file from the storage medium; instead it replaces the first character of the file name in the directory with a character that indicates that the space is available for rewriting. Before such rewriting occurs, the file is available for recovery.

unfragmented. A hard disk that has its files in consecutive sectors. When the disk is first written to, files are stored in consecutive sectors. As files are erased and replaced, the replacement file is stored in whatever sectors are first available. After awhile, a file will occupy a number of widely separated sectors, which slows file reading and causes additional wear and tear on the head because of the additional head movement needed to position the head at each of the widely separated sectors. The disk is then said to be *fragmented*.

uniform. Having equally spaced subdivisions.

unimodular transform. A matrix with integral weights and a unit determinant that relates equivalent lattices.

union. In constructive solid geometry, a region in space that is within at least one of two or more specified objects.

universal product code. (UPC). A standard bar code applied to the packages of retail products. A reader for this code can convert it into pulses that are read by a computer. It is used to keep track of inventory, sales, etc.

UNIX. A multiuser/multitasking computer operating system developed originally and trademarked by AT&T. It is available in versions to work with many different computer architectures.

unzip. To decompress a file that has been compressed with the *PKZIP* compression program by using the *PKUNZIP* program.

UPC. Universal product code. A standard bar code applied to the packages of retail products. A reader for this code can convert it into pulses that are read by a computer. It is used to keep track of inventory, sales, etc.

update rate. The rate at which a new image is displayed on a monitor screen. Contrast to *refresh rate* which is the rate at which an image is redrawn on the screen regardless of whether it is the same or a new image.

UQUM. Use quick update methods. A command in the PHIGS system that initiates fast erase and repaint techniques that may have minor imperfections. When such imperfections have accumulated to the point where the image is severely degraded, it must be completely regenerated.

UVN coordinate system. A coordinate system used in ray tracing that is based on the viewing plane.

V

valuator device. A computer device that inputs absolute numbers rather than relative data such as produced by a track ball or mouse. First used as GKS terminology.

value. A property of a color that is proportional to the brightness of the light impinging on the colored object.

vaporware. Software whose availability has been announced and which has possibly been demonstrated, but is not currently available to customers (often because it contains too many bugs for commercial use).

variable length record. A record in a data base that may vary in length, depending upon the data stored in it. Reading variable length records requires more sophisticated software than is needed to read fixed length records.

VCR. Video cassette recorder. A device for the recording and playback of television signals on magnetic tape.

VDM. Virtual device metafile. An ANSI/ISO standard currently under development that will be used to establish formats for direct communication of graphics primitives from computers to display devices, printers, and plotters. Also known as *computer graphics interface*.

vec. An arbitrary-size one-dimensional array of real numbers.

vector. A straight line defined by the coordinates of its endpoints.

vector display. A monitor that displays images using vectored line segments rather than pixel-by-pixel writing.

vector dither. A dithering technique that uses a dither matrix that is not fixed in screen space, but instead is oriented along the length of a line.

vector quantization. An image compression technique in which the image is encoded as a sequence of addresses to a table of small blocks of pixels which are relatively close representations of blocks of pixels in the original image. The name comes from the concept of each block of pixels as representing the components of a vector and attempting to find vectors that are close together.

vectorgraphic displays. Displays, usually of the flat panel type, which are characterized by having individually addressable pixels.

vectorization. Translation of a bit-mapped image into an image defined by vectors.

verification suite. A formal set of tests developed to verify that a program meets all of its specifications. Essential to assure that program modifications do not introduce secondary bugs.

verso. In typography, the left-hand page of a book or magazine. The right-hand page is called *recto*.

vertex. A point which marks the intersection of two or more edges of a polygon or other graphics object.

vertex normal. A normal vector at a vertex of a graphics object. Rather than being normal to one of the intersecting surfaces, it is normal to the average of the surface normals of all of the intersecting surfaces.

vertical recording. A magnetic disk recording technique that records pulses into the media rather than across it. This permits a higher density of stored data.

vertical resolution. 1. The number of scanlines that are visible on a monitor display screen. 2. The number of horizontal lines that can be reproduced by a video camera and monitor combination.

vertical retrace. The portion of a video signal during which the scanning electron beam is moved from the end of one field to the beginning of the next. Video is usually blanked during *vertical retrace* so that retrace lines do not appear on the screen.

vertical scan frequency. The rate, in hertz, at which the display image frame is refreshed.

very high density. (VHD). A technique for recording 20 megabytes of data on a 3½-inch magnetic disk.

very large scale integration. (VLSI). A technique for placing thousands of active elements on an integrated circuit chip.

VESA. Video Electronics Standards Association. A body that sets video standards.

vesicular film. A film similar to diazo film that uses diazo salts. It is used to make copies of microfilm originals.

VGA. Video Graphics Array. An IBM video display graphics standard card. It is capable of 640 pixel × 480 pixel × 16 color and 320 pixel × 200 pixel × 256 color displays.

VHD. Very high density. A technique for recording 20 megabytes of data on a 3½-inch magnetic disk.

VHS. (™ Japan Victor Corp). Video home system. A format for recording television signals on half-inch tape cassettes.

video. A sequence of electronic signals that can be transformed into animated images for viewing on a display screen.

video camera. A camera that can accept a light image and convert it into a television signal.

video cassette recorder. (VCR). A device for the recording and playback of television signals on magnetic tape.

video codec. Electronic circuitry for converting an analog video signal into digital code.

video digitizer. A device that converts a video picture into a digital file. Also known as a *frame grabber.*

video mode. A selection of screen resolution and number of available display colors from an IBM or clone graphics adapter card.

video random access memory. (VRAM). A type of random access memory in which each address can be accessed individually by the computer, but the memory can be treated as a shift register for reading data to the display device.

Video Electronics Standards Association. (VESA). A body that sets video standards.

Video Graphics Array. (VGA). An IBM video display graphics standard card. It is capable of 640 pixel × 480 pixel × 16 color and 320 pixel × 200 pixel × 256 color displays.

videodisk. A read-only optical disk that holds up to two hours of analog video data and permits instant access to any place on the disk.

videotex. A display that is a combination of text and simple, locally rendered graphics that is produced by a low bandwidth stream of encoded drawing commands, permitting transmission over low bandwidth devices such as phone lines.

viewing coordinates. A coordinate system that is centered at the viewpoint of a scene.

viewing geometry. The geometry involved in viewing a scene from some observer's viewpoint with a display screen interposed between the viewer and the scene.

viewpoint. The coordinates of a point at which a camera or the human eye is situated in viewing a scene.

virtual device metafile. (VDM). An ANSI/ISO standard currently under development that will be used to establish formats for direct communication of graphics primitives from computers to display devices, printers, and plotters. Also known as *computer graphics interface*.

virtual reality. A simulation that includes stereo vision, with the observed scene coordinated with head movement of the observer; stereo sound; and the ability to control certain parts of the display through the movements of the hand within a special glove. Term coined by Jaron Lanier.

visibility algorithm. In scene rendering graphics, a method for determining whether a point is visible from the observer's viewpoint.

visual acuity. The maximum resolution of the human eye. This occurs at the center of the eye; resolution falls off toward the edges. The maximum is about 1 milliradian.

visual computing. Software methods for creating and displaying graphics images.

visualization. The creation of computer graphics images that display data for human interpretation. Particularly useful for multidimensional scientific data.

vivid. A color that is nearly pure, having a high degree of color saturation.

VLSI. Very large scale integration. A technique for placing thousands of active elements on an integrated circuit chip.

volatile storage. Computer memory (such as RAM) which is erased when computer power is turned off.

volume label. A name of up to 11 characters (in MS-DOS) that may be assigned to a floppy or hard disk.

volume rendering. The producing of an image that shows the spatial relationships of a three-dimensional data set.

Voronoi diagram. A structure used to map colors in the RGB color space.

voxel. One of an array of equal-sized cubes that comprise a discretely defined three-dimensional space.

VRAM. Video random access memory. A type of random access memory in which each address can be individually accessed by the computer, but the memory can be treated as a shift register for reading data to the display device.

VST. A file format for storing a color graphics image. It is an extension of the TGA format.

W

WAC window. Wide area collimating window. An assembly consisting of a beam splitter and a curved mirror that is used to enlarge the image on a cathode-ray tube.

wallpaper. A background pattern, often consisting of a tiling by a small geometric pattern.

wand. A hand-held scanning device used for reading bar codes or for optical character reading.

Warnock's algorithm. A solution of the hidden surface problem (the determining of which object surfaces are visible and which are occluded) by recursively subdividing the image area until in each subdivision a single polygon is found to be occluding all other polygons that are in that subdivision.

warping. 1. The two-dimensional mapping of an image to produce an image for display. 2. The distorting of an image to give an unusual effect. The technique used produces the same results as if the image were on a sheet of rubber that is stretched in some areas and compressed in others. It is accomplished by remapping the pixels of the image using affine transformations that are determined by the relation of each original pixel to some established control points. Often *warping* is used in association with animation, with the image being slowly distorted from its original shape to the final shape over a period of time.

waterfall. A technique for producing an image where the gray-scale intensity of the image is proportional to height. Also known as a *fuzzy rug*.

wave. A periodic disturbance that travels through a medium. It has a frequency and amplitude.

Weber's law. The fact that a just noticeable increase in sensation depends on the ratio of the increase to the original stimulus.

weight.   In typography, the thickness of strokes of a character in proportion to the height of the typeface. The weight determines whether a font is classified as light, regular, bold, etc.

Weiler-Atherton algorithm.   A solution of the hidden surface problem (the determining of which object surfaces are visible and which are occluded) by subdividing the image area along polygon boundaries until in each subdivision a single polygon is found to be occluding all other polygons that are in that subdivision.

weld.   To convert vertices that are in close proximity to a common set of coordinates to eliminate cracking. The assumption is that these vertices are close enough so that the differences in their coordinates are due to computer round-off or accuracy errors and that they are actually all the same vertex.

white level.   The upper limit for television signals or display image color values, corresponding to the brightest color white.

white noise.   Noise whose power is constant across the frequency spectrum.

white space.   In typography, white space left on a page to give the page a pleasing appearance.

whitening filter.   A filter used to increase the white content of a colored area.

Whitted's method.   A technique for deriving refraction formulas.

WID.   Window identifier. An attribute stored with each pixel of an image which may, for example, be used to identify the associated window or color mode.

WID RAM.   Window identifier random access memory. A table of color modes or window identifiers used to decode WID values on output.

wide area collimating window.   (WAC window). An assembly consisting of a beam splitter and a curved mirror that is used to enlarge the image on a cathode-ray tube.

widow.   A word or short line that ends a paragraph.

width table. A table stored in a word processor or other publishing software which lists all of the characters in a font and their widths.

wildcard. A character used in text searching which is considered a match for any character in that position. For example, a search for *abc.???* where *?* is the wildcard would be satisfied by *abc.dir, abc.wxy,* or any other combination that begins with *abc*.

Winchester disk. A sealed hard disk unit. The name is derived from the Winchester rifle, since the original *Winchester disk* developed by IBM was for the 3030 computer system.

winding rule. A method for finding whether a point is inside or outside a polygon by summing the angles with respect to the point.

window identifier. (WID). An attribute stored with each pixel of an image which may, for example, be used to identify the associated window or color mode.

window identifier random access memory. (WID RAM). A table of color modes or window identifiers used to decode WID values on output.

Windows. A multi-screen graphical user interface system developed by MicroSoft which sits as a shell over MS-DOS.

wire printer. A dot matrix printer that uses a column of wire hammers to strike a ribbon and in turn produce ink dots on a sheet of paper.

wireframe modeling. A graphics modeling technique in which graphics objects are represented by an array of polygons and only the edges of the polygons are drawn.

wobulator. A technique for widening the raster line of a cathode-ray tube display by modulating the deflection in an orthogonal direction at a much higher rate than the line scan frequency.

word processing or **wordprocessing.** Software that allows entry, editing, manipulation, formatting, and printing of text.

word wrapping. The automatic insertion of carriage return and line feed by a word processor when the end of a line is reached in inputting text. Also known as *wraparound*.

workstation. A single-user computer, usually of high performance and with a high-resolution display. A workstation is usually designed primarily for high performance with little attention being given to ease of use.

world coordinates. A coordinate system used to define the three-dimensional space in which a scene occurs.

worldwide phosphor type designation system. (WTDS). A universal system for designating the phosphors used on the face of cathode-ray tubes.

WORM. Write once read many. An optical storage device having a medium on which data can be written only once, but may be read as often as desired.

WPM. A file extension denoting an object-oriented graphics file compatible with the Microsoft Windows system.

wraparound. The automatic insertion of carriage return and line feed by a word processor when the end of a line is reached in inputting text. Also known as *word wrapping*.

wrapping. Wraparound.

write once read many. (WORM). An optical storage device having a medium on which data can be written only once, but may be read as often as desired.

write protect. A method of preventing writing to a magnetic disk. A 3½-inch floppy disk is *write protected* by moving a small button at the top right of the disk; a 5¼-inch floppy disk is *write protected* by covering a notch in the disk envelope with a small metallic tape.

wrong reading. Reading an image from right to left.

WTDS. Worldwide phosphor type designation system. A universal system for designating the phosphors used on the face of cathode-ray tubes.

Wu's algorithm. An algorithm used to perform color quantization.

WYSIWYG.   What you see is what you get. A display for a word processing or publishing program that uses graphics to represent the size and shape of text characters as closely as possible so that the displayed page will be nearly identical to the corresponding printed page.

X

x axis. The horizontal axis of a two-dimensional cartesian coordinate system. Increasing positive values of x move to the right.

X terminal. A display device for receiving input, displaying text and graphics, and transmitting keyboard output from an X Window System.

X Window System. A window operating system developed at the Massachusetts Institute of Technology for use in networked UNIX applications. It is now also available for PCs and is widely used as an industry standard.

X.11. The eleventh version of the X Windows System.

X.25. A standards recommendation for packet switched communications over a network. Developed by CCITT.

x-height. The height of a lowercase x in a given type font. A method of measuring type size.

X-on/X-off. A technique for serial transmission of data to a device that cannot accept data as fast as the transmission rate. When the receiving device has accepted all information that it can store and process, it sends an *X-off* character to the transmitter, which then pauses. When the receiver is ready to accept more data, it sends an *X-on* character to the transmitter which then begins sending data again.

X3H3. The particular American National Standards Committee concerned with graphics specifications.

XDR. External data representation. A technique for sharing data over a network among different computers.

xerography. A printing technology in which an image is formed by an electrostatic charge on a special metallic drum. The charged portions of the drum then pick up toner which is transferred to a sheet of paper and fused permanently by heat. Used for copiers and laser printers.

XGA. Extended graphics adapter. An IBM standard graphics adapter that supports resolutions up to 1024 pixels × 768 pixels.

XMIT. To transmit.

XOR. The exclusive OR logic function. When two inputs are alike, a one is output; when they are different, a zero is output.

XT. The designation of the IBM PC/XT personal computer, the first IBM personal computer to have a hard disk. Also applied to clones having similar characteristics and using an 8088 microprocessor.

x-y plotter. A plotter that plots using cartesian coordinates.

xyY space. A three-dimensional space for defining colors based on the CIE system. The x component is the chromacity and the y component is the luminance. The z component need not be defined, since in this system the sum of the x, y, and z components is one.

XYZ space. The CIE three-dimensional coordinate space for defining colors.

Y

Y. The luminance component of a color video signal encoded in the YIQ color space.

y axis. The vertical axis of a two-dimensional cartesian coordinate system. Normally increasing positive values of *y* move upward, but in most computer graphics displays, the origin is at the top left corner of the screen and increasing positive values of *y* move downward.

yaw. Periodic angular displacement of a vehicle about the vertical axis in the plane of the longitudinal and lateral axes.

yellow. One of the four subtractive process colors that are used in four-color printing.

YIQ space. A three-dimensional space for defining colors. The three orthogonal axes are *Y*, the luminance or brightness component; *I*, the in-phase signal, which is orange-cyan; and *Q*, the quadrature signal, which is green-magenta. The space is designed so that the *I* (in-phase signal) by itself produces an acceptable black and white picture.

YMCK. Yellow, magenta, cyan, and key (for black). The four subtractive colors used in color printing. All colors in a picture are comprised of these four basic colors. Color printing is accomplished by four passes through the printing press, each pass using ink of one of these basic colors. (More commonly known as *CMYK*.)

yon. A clipping plane perpendicular to the line of sight that is used to eliminate rendering of objects that are too far distant to be of interest in a scene. 2. The distance from the viewpoint to the *yon* clipping plane along the line of sight.

Z

z.   In rendering a graphics image, the distance perpendicular to the display (image) plane from an object to a plane parallel to the display plane through the viewpoint.

z axis.   The depth axis in a three-dimensional cartesian coordinate system.

zap.   To wipe out a file, usually accidentally.

Zapf dingbats.   A particular font of *dingbats* (nonalphanumeric symbols) created by typeface designer Hermann Zapf and copyright by International Type Corporation.

z-buffer.   A two-dimensional array made up of a grid of points on a sea-level plane, each containing the value of the height (z) at that point.

zero.   The numeral meaning nothing. In computer printouts, it is often written as an *0* with a slash through it to distinguish it from the capital letter *O*.

zero phase filter.   A filter that uses an odd number of samples, thereby producing an output that is situated at the same location as the middle input sample. Compare with *half phase filter*.

zip.   To compress a file using the *PKZIP* program.

zoom.   To enlarge a portion of an image so that it fills the entire screen.

zoom pyramid.   A sequence of digital images starting with a high-resolution image and continuing with lower-resolution images, each of which has one-half the resolution of the previous image. Requires only one-third more storage than the high-resolution image and permits the display of an image of any desired resolution, either directly or through interpolation.

Appendix

Manufacturers of Graphics Equipment

Graphics Adapter Cards

Actix Systems, Inc.
3060 Tasman Dr.
Santa Clara, CA 95054
Phone: (800) 927-5557

Artist Graphics Inc.
2675 Patton Rd.
St. Paul, MN 55113
Phone: (612) 631-7800

ATI Technologies Inc.
3761 Victoria Park Avenue
Scarborough, Ontario, Canada M1W 3S2
Phone: (416) 756-0718

Boca Research
6413 Congress Ave.
Boca Raton, FL 33487
Phone: (407) 997-6227

Cache Computers, Inc.
46600 Landing Parkway
Fremont, CA 94538
Phone: (510) 226-9922

Cardinal Technologies, Inc.
1827 Freedom Rd.
Lancaster, PA 17601
Phone: (800) 233-0187

Diamond Computer Systems, Inc.
532 Mercury Drive
Sunnyvale, CA 94086
Phone: (408) 736-2000

Edge Technology, Inc.
915 E. Karcher Rd.
Nampa, ID 83687-3045
Phone: (800) 438-3343

Focus Information Systems, Inc.
4046 Clipper Court
Fremont, CA 94538
Phone: (800) 925-2378

Hercules Computer Technology, Inc.
921 Parker St.
Berkeley, CA 94710
Phone: (800) 532-0600

IOcomm International Technology Corp.
12700 Yukon Ave.
Hawthorne, CA 90250
Phone: (800) 998-8919

Kingston Technology Corp.
17600 Newhope St.
Fountain Valley, CA 92708
Phone: (800) 835-6375

Matrox Electronic Systems Ltd.
1055 St. Regis Blvd.
Dorval, Quebec, Canada H9P 2T4
Phone: (800) 462-8769

Metheus Corp.
1600 NW Compton Dr.
Beaverton, OR 97006-6905
Phone: (503) 690-1550

Mylex Corp.
34551 Ardenwood Blvd.
Fremont, CA 94555-3607
Phone: (800) 77-MYLEX

National Design Inc.
1515 Capital of Texas Highway South
5th Floor
Austin, TX 78746
Phone: (512) 329-5055

Orchid Technology
45365 Northport Loop
West Fremont, CA 94538
Phone: (800) 767-2443

Paradise (Western Digital Corp.)
8105 Irvine Center Dr.
Irvine, CA 92718
Phone: (714) 932-4900

Pixelworks Inc.
7 Park Ave.
Hudson, NH 03051
Phone: (800) 247-2476

Portacom Technologies Inc.
800 El Camino Real West #251
Mountain View, CA 94040
Phone: (415) 390-8504

Presenta Technologies Corp.
12806 Schabarum Ave. Unit F
Irwindale, CA 91706
Phone: (818) 960-0430

Prism Imaging Systems
5309 Randall Pl.
Fremont, CA 94538
Phone: (408) 280-7029

Pycon Inc.
3501 Leonard Ct.
Santa Clara, CA 95034
Phone: (800) 435-7999

Quickpath Systems Inc.
46723 Fremont Blvd.
Fremont, CA 94538
Phone: (510) 440-7288

Sigma Designs, Inc.
47900 Bayside Parkway
Fremont, CA 94538
Phone: (800) 845-8086

STB Systems, Inc.
P. O. Box 850957
Richardson, TX 75083-0957
Phone: (214) 234-8750

Tangram Technology Corp.
3087 No. First St.
San Jose, CA 95134
Phone: (408) 428-9165

Trident Microsystems, Inc.
321 Soquel Way
Sunnyvale, CA 95125
Phone: (408) 738-3194

Tseng Labs Inc.
6 Terry Dr.
Newtown, PA 18940
Phone: (215) 968-0502

Video Seven (Headlands Technology Inc.)
46305 Landing Parkway
Fremont, CA 94538
Phone: (800) 238-0101

VidTech Microsystems Inc.
1700 93rd Lane, NE
Minneapolis, MN 55449
Phone: (800) 752-8033

Monitors

Acer America Corp.
2641 Orchard Parkway
San Jose, CA 95134
Phone: (800) 733-2237

American Milac Corp.
410 E. Plumeria Dr.
San Jose, CA 95134
Phone: (800) 648-2287

CTX International Inc.
20530 Earlgate St.
Walnut, CA 91789
Phone: (714) 595-6146

Epson America Inc.
20770 Madrona Ave.
Torrance, CA 90503
Phone: (800) 922-8911

Goldstar Technology, Inc.
1130 E. Arques Ave.
Sunnyvale, CA 94086
Phone: (408) 432-1331

Hewlett-Packard Co.
California Personal Computer Division
974 E. Arques Ave.
P. O. Box 3486
Sunnyvale, CA 94086
Phone: (800) 752-0900

Hitachi America, Ltd.
220 White Plains Rd.
Tarrytown, NY 10591
Phone: (914) 631-0600

Idek/Iiyama North America Inc.
650 Louis Dr. #120
Warminster, PA 18974
Phone: (215) 957-6543

MAG Inovision Inc.
4392 Corporate Center Dr.
Los Alamitos, CA 90720
Phone: (800) 827-3998

Magnavox (N.A.P. Consumer Electronics Corp.)
P. O. Box 555
Jefferson City, TN 37760
Phone: (615) 475-3801

Mitsubishi Electronics America, Inc.
Information Systems Division
5757 Plaza Drive
P. O. Box 6007
Cypress, CA 90630
Phone: (800) 843-2515

Nanao USA Corp.
23535 Telo Ave.
Torrance, CA 90505
Phone: (800) 800-5202

NEC Technologies Inc.
1255 Michael Dr.
Wood Dale, IL 60191
Phone: (800) 388-8888

Packard Bell
9425 Canoga Ave.
Chatsworth, CA 91311
Phone: (800) 521-7979

Panasonic Communications and Systems Co.
2 Panasonic Way
Secaucus, NJ 07094
Phone: (201) 392-6313

Samsung Electronic Devices
14251 E. Firestone Bl. No. 101
La Mirada, CA 90638
Phone: (213) 802-8425

Seiko Instruments USA, Inc.
1130 Ringwood Ct.
San Jose, CA 95131
Phone: (800) 888-0817

Sony Computer Peripheral Products Co.
655 River Oaks Parkway
San Jose, CA 95134
Phone: (800) 352-7669

Tatung Co. of America Inc.
2850 El Presido St.
Long Beach, CA 90810
Phone: (800) 829-2850

Toshiba America Consumer Products Inc.
1010 Johnson Dr.
Buffalo Grove, IL 60089
Phone: (800) 253-5429

ViewSonic
12130 Mora Dr.
Santa Fe Springs, CA 90670
Phone: (800) 888-8583

Zenith Data Systems
1000 Milwaukee Ave.
Glenview, IL 60025
Phone: (800) 842-9000

Printers

Alps Electric (USA), Inc.
3553 N. First St.
San Jose, CA 95134
Phone: (408) 432-6035

Apple Computer Co.
20525 Mariani Ave.
Cupertino, CA 95014
Phone: (800) 776-2333

Brother International Corp. USA
200 Cottontail Ln.
Somerset, NJ 08875
Phone: (800) 284-4357

C. Itoh (C-Tech Electronics Inc.)
2515 McCabe Way
Irvine, CA 92713
Phone: (800) 347-4017

Canon U.S.A.
1 Canon Plaza
Lake Success, NY 11042
Phone: (516) 354-1114

Citizen (CBM America Corp.)
2020 Santa Monica Blvd. Suite 410
Santa Monica, CA 90404
Phone: (213) 828-8245

Epson America Inc.
20770 Madrona Ave.
Torrance, CA 90503
Phone: (800) 922-8911

Fujitsu America, Inc.
2904 Orchard Parkway
San Jose, CA 95134
Phone: (800) 626-4686

Hewlett-Packard Co.
P. O. Box 8059
Santa Clara, CA 95051
Phone: (800) 752-0900

Kyocera Electronics Inc.
100 Randolph Rd.
Somerset, NJ 08875
Phone: (908) 560-3400

LaserMaster Corp.
6900 Shady Oak Rd.
Eden Prairie, MN 55344
Phone: (800) 950-6868

IBM (LexMark International Inc.)
740 New Circle Rd.
Lexington, KY 40511
Phone: (800) 426-2468

NEC Technologies Inc.
1414 Massachusetts Ave.
Boxborough, MA 01719
Phone: (800) 388-8888

Okidata
532 Fellowship Rd.
Mount Laurel, NJ 08504
Phone: (800) 654-3282

Panasonic Communications and Systems Co.
2 Panasonic Way
Secaucus, NJ 07094
Phone: (800) 742-8086

Samsung Electronics America Inc.
Information Systems Division
105 Challenger Rd.
Ridgefield Park, NJ 07660
Phone: (800) 446-0262

Texas Instruments Inc.
P. O. Box 202230
Auston, TX 78720-2230
Phone: (800) 527-3500

Toshiba America Information Systems Inc.
Electronic Imaging Division
9740 Irvine Blvd.
Irvine, CA 92718
Phone: (800) 468-6744

Xante Corp.
2559 Emogene St.
Mobile, AL 36606
Phone: (800) 926-8839

Other Academic Press Professional Titles of Interest

Modern Image Processing: Warping, Morphing, and Classical Techniques
by Christopher D. Watkins, Alberto Sadun, and Stephen Marenka

Image Processing has applications to numerous disciplines, and with the availability of powerful and inexpensive hardware, it is now an area being implemented and investigated by all levels of computer users. *Modern Image Processing* contains both practical and theoretical information regarding techniques for processing images that are scanned or take through a CCD (camera array-digital camera). It instructs the reader about how to enhance, manipulate, and extract information from the images which have been acquired. The book also includes the source code required to perform all of the image manipulation.

ISBN 0-12-737860-X   August, 1993; $49.95

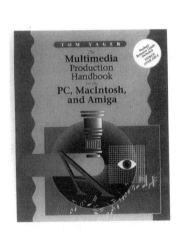

Multimedia Production Handbook for the PC, Macintosh, and Amiga
by Tom Yager

This handbook is a comprehensive resource guide for selecting an appropriate multimedia system from among the many currently available. It focuses on three of the best platforms for Multimedia applications: IBM, Macintosh, and Amiga. Author Tom Yager brings two years of experience as director of Byte Magazine's Multimedia Lab to this exciting new text. By using this book, managers, developers, and end-users can more effectively map out their time and capital for resources and development.

ISBN 0-12-768030-6   August, 1993; $35.95 (tentative)

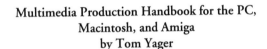

Usability Engineering
by Jakob Nielsen

Written by the author of the best-selling *Hypertext & Hypermedia*, this book offers an excellent introduction to Usability Engineering. Practical guidelines for addressing usability considerations in the software engineering process are covered throughout the book. It also provides concrete advice and methods that can be systematically implemented to ensure a high level of usability in the final interface.

ISBN 0-12-518405-2   April 1993; $29.95

Other Academic Press Professional Titles of Interest

Going from C to C++
by Robert Traister

Going from C to C++ introduces the ins and outs of C++ within a framework of ANSI C (the standard C language). As the book explores the new tools offered by C++, it also relies on the programmer's knowledge of ANSI C, providing a logical evolution in C++ programming. Bob Traister uses his expertise as a software "test site" for major corporations to gently guide the reader through the transition process. The book also includes a 5 1/4" disk for 286 or higher IBM compatibles containing source code for all working programs and modules in the book.

ISBN 0-12-697412-8   April 1993; $34.95

Virtual Reality: Applications and Explorations
edited by Alan Wexelblat

Virtual Reality: Applications and Explorations collects original essays, including contributions from some of the leaders in the field, that illustrate the myriad and potentially powerful applications of virtual reality. These essays examine a broad range of practical applications of virtual reality, from entertainment and architectural design to teleconferencing and computer-supported cooperative work. Researchers at the forefront of work in this area explain the capabilities of some present systems and then outline the even more compelling possibilities they envision. From developing advanced interfaces for education in the classroom to visualizing scientific data for simulated space exploration, the essays make clear the diverse ways that virtual environments can be useful as tools and suggest exciting directions for the future.

ISBN 0-12-745045-9   August, 1993; $39.95

Other Academic Press Professional Titles of Interest

T$_E$XHelp: The On-Line T$_E$X Handbook
by Arvind Borde

This innovative package gives T$_E$X users access to on-line help with most aspects of the program. It supplies explanations of all T$_E$X commands, and it discusses a large range of typesetting topics.

The program:

- is a useful tool for the beginning and advanced T$_E$X user
- is completely menu driven and is very easy to use
- works like a HyperText tool: entries contain highlighted words that users can choose in order to directly access further information
- allows users to save entries in files, which can be processed with T$_E$X and printed or previewed
- permits, on some systems, direct T$_E$X previewing of entries by pressing a single key.

The package provides a data file which contains descriptions and explanations of T$_E$X commands, as well as discussions of many commonly-used typesetting terms and techniques. It also provides a file of new T$_E$X commands that allows the processing and previewing of saved entries.

This program was developed by Arvind Borde with the assistance of Tomas Rokicki.

ISBN 0-12-117640-1 $49.95 (tentative)

Using C in Software Design
by Ronald Leach

Using C in Software Design provides a creative approach to learning C by emphasizing software engineering. This text is designed for beginners or those learning C as a second language. ANSI C is used throughout the book and thought-provoking problems are included at the end of each chapter. The book is divided into two sections; the first emphasizes the simpler software engineering aspects of C, allowing the reader to begin writing interesting programs quickly. The second part discusses advanced C topics, such as pointers, structures, and the design of larger C programs which extend over several source code files.

ISBN 0-12-440210-0   August, 1993; $39.95 (tentative)

Other Academic Press Professional Titles of Interest

FRACTALS EVERYWHERE
Second Edition
Michael F. Barnsley

ISBN 0-12-079061-0

June 1993

$49.95

560 pp.

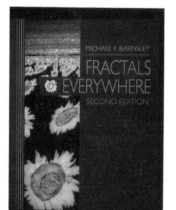

About the Second Edition:

"The material contained in the second edition is quite obviously more extensive in detail and scope....the style of writing is technically excellent, informative, and entertaining....the material in this book will make an excellent university-level course."

— Robert McCarty

"The problems and examples are well-chosen and interesting....difficult concepts are introduced in a clear fashion with excellent diagrams and graphs."

— Alan E. Wessel
Santa Clara University

This volume is the second edition of the highly successful *Fractals Everywhere*. The focus of this text is how fractal geometry can be used to model real objects in the physical world. The new edition features:

• A new chapter on Recurrent Iterated Function Systems, including Vector Recurrent Iterated Functions (V-RIFs)™

• Problems and tools emphasizing fractal applications

• An all-new answer key to problems in the text, with solutions and hints.

This edition of *Fractals Everywhere* is the most complete and up-to-date fractal textbook available today.

Fractals Everywhere may be supplemented by Michael F. Barnsley's *Desktop Fractal Design System* (version 2.0) with IBM or Macintosh software. *The Desktop Fractal Design System 2.0* is a tool for designing Iterated Function Systems codes and fractal images, and makes an excellent supplement to a course on fractal geometry.

Other Academic Press Professional Titles of Interest

Radiosity and Realistic Image Synthesis
by Michael Cohen and John Wallace

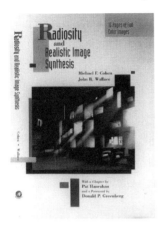

Radiosity and Realistic Image Synthesis is the first comprehensive look at the radiosity method and the tools required for creating visual experiences via the computer. Basic concepts and mathematical fundamentals underlying image synthesis and radiosity algorithms are covered thoroughly (a basic knowledge of undergraduate calculus is assumed). Discussions are based on algorithms developed to implement the radiosity method, ranging from environment subdivision to final displays. Successes and obstacles in implementing these algorithms are highlighted. Over 100 illustrations and 16 pages of full-color images explain the developments and results of the radiosity method.

ISBN 0-12-178270-0   July, 1993; $49.95

HYPERSTAT
Macintosh Hypermedia for Analyzing Data and Learning Statistics
by David M. Lane

HyperStat is a unique hypermedia software package for the Macintosh. It serves as an integrated combination of a program for data analysis, a hypertext in statistics, and a set of interactive simu-

lation/data exercises called "explorations." It is both a statistics book that can do calculations and a statistical analysis system with a tremendous amount of on-line help. A 120 page user manual is also included.

HyperStat's statistical procedures cover simple as well as more sophisticated analyses. For instance, *HyperStat* has procedures for multiple regression and complex analysis of variance. The latter procedure can compute an analysis of variance with up to four between-subject variables. Other procedures emphasize graphics such as box plots, stem and leaf plots, scatterplots, frequency polygons, and histograms.

HyperStat uses hypertext to provide over 2,000 links between related concepts and between results of statistical analyses and explanatory material. The combination of hypertext and *HyperStat's* electronic index makes looking up information extremely easy.

ISBN: 0-12-436130-7   July 1993; $59.95

ORDER FORM

To Order: Return this form with your payment to Academic Press, Inc., Order Fulfillment Department, 6277 Sea Harbor Drive, Orlando, FL 32821-9816 or
call toll-free 1-800-321-5068

QUANTITY	AUTHOR/TITLE	ISBN	PRICE
		Subtotal	
		Sales Tax (where applicable)	
		TOTAL	

☐ Payment enclosed (please include applicable tax)

☐ Bill me directly (We cannot ship to a P.O. box)*

☐ Bill my company (purchase order attached)*
*Shipping, handling, and tax will be added to billed orders. Tax will be added to credit card orders.

Charge Card #_____ Expiration Date_____

Your Signature_____

Name_____ Telephone _____

Address_____

City_____ State/Country_____

Zip/Postal Code_____